Martine Briat - Jean-Paul Grimaud
Yannick De Oliveira - Jean-Charles Varennes

Wonderful
AUVERGNE

Translated by Angela Moyon

ÉDITIONS OUEST-FRANCE
13, rue du Breil, Rennes

*Four symbolic pictures of Auvergne :
Top to bottom :
- Puy de Dôme, the view from a
hang-glider;
- white water near Le Monastier-
sur-Gazeille (Haute-Loire);
- the pre-Romanesque church in
Neuville-près-Billom (Puy-de-Dôme).*

*Opposite page : Tournoël Castle
near Riom (Puy-de-Dôme).*

*Front cover : Murol Castle and the
Monts Dore range.*

*Back cover : Saint-Michel d'Aiguilhe
Rock in Le Puy-en-Velay (Haute-
Loire).*

© 1991, Édilarge S.A. - Éditions Ouest-France, Rennes

A BRIEF LOOK AT HISTORY

Although the Massif Central was ignored by the first waves of settlers, the Limagne Corridor, like the areas in which the soil was light or the rock shelters created by lava flows, were used by man very early on in his existence.

It would seem that certain places in the Velay and Allier Valley were occupied as far back as two million years ago.

The Stone Age has left numerous traces in Auvergne, e.g. axes, arrow heads, and a miscellany of tools. After the end of the Campignian and Chassean Eras, the Stone Age left a legacy of standing stones in the form of dolmens, menhirs and barrows.

The Bronze and, later, the Iron Ages, ranging from the Hallstatt civilisation to La Tène, were particularly brilliant in Auvergne, and numerous archaeological treasures having been found in the barrow graves of Cantal or in a number of hillforts (Corent, Puy-de-Dôme).

The Arverni civilisation reached its peak in the 3rd century B.C., when its authority extended far beyond the borders of the region. Its importance was shown by the fact that it minted its own gold coins.

Julius Caesar's conquest of Gaul was momentarily halted by the victorious resistance put up by Vercingetorix, initially in Gergovia, although the exact site of the battle has given rise to many a controversy between local experts.

Once Caesar had triumphed, the Arverni region became a flourishing Roman province. Place names show extensive Roman presence in the Limagnes, Velay or Bourbonnais area, where the suffixes -ac, -at, or -ieux are common.

Many of the major Gallo-Roman sanctuaries were built on sites that still exist. A Temple of Mercury, for example, was built on the summit of the Puy de Dôme and Cantal had a polygonal Temple of Aron. Large towns developed, such as *Augustonemetum* (Clermont-Ferrand), *Ruessium* (Saint-Paulien, Haute-Loire). In the 1st century B.C., Lezoux was the capital of Roman sigillated pottery. In Allier, digs have revealed traces of villas and baths.

3

A fresco in the castle in Saint-Floret (Puy-de-Dôme).

By the 5th century A.D., the Roman civilisation was beginning to fade. In Clermont, Sidoine Appolinaire opposed Euric. In the Bourbonnais region, Ebreuil was laid to waste and Cordès razed to the ground.

This marked the beginning of a troubled period during which Auvergne swung between the Dukes of Aquitaine, the Merovingians and the Carolingians.

There are a few, meagre traces of the Saracen invasion in Clermont-Ferrand, or near Billom (Puy-de-Dôme), and of the later Viking invasions which resulted in the burning down of Clermont-Ferrand.

In the Velay region, the beginnings of Christianity led to the removal of the bishopric from Saint-Paulien to Le Puy (5th century). Thereafter, the town enjoyed constant expansion and development. The pilgrimage to Notre-Dame became one of the main spiritual experiences in the Christian Western World. Moreover, as the starting point of one of the roads to Santiago de Compostela, the town's influence spread throughout Europe. In Allier, there were increasing numbers of saints. The museums are filled with reminders of this intense religious feeling (Gannat gospels, font in Massigny etc.).

Within this atmosphere of weak rulers and latent anarchy, an entire network of forts was built in Auvergne, from primitive feudal mottes topped by the earliest wooden forts, to the sophisticated castles of the 11th century. Later, military architecture developed from the square or quadrangle to a circular layout that was a more efficient form of defence because it did not leave any blind angles.

It takes the eye of an expert to distinguish the remains of feudal mottes, but visitors are always surprised at the number of "eagle's nests" on hilltops, in a more or less advanced state of ruin after the passing of the years.

In the mid 13th century, the "great century" of the Middle Ages, Auvergne was governed by Alphonse of Poitiers, St. Louis' brother. The region was managed by a constable who was resident in Riom. The upper Auvergne (Cantal) was then entrusted to the care of a "Bailiff of the Mountains of Auvergne".

Numerous franchises were granted to towns or villages during this period (Maringues in Limagne, Besse and Riom in Puy-de-Dôme, Saint-Flour and Salers in Cantal, and Le Puy-en-Velay).

After this period of peace and prosperity, Auvergne was subjected, in the mid 14th century, to adversities such as the Great Plague of 1348 and the One Hundred Years' War. It may not have been the scene of any major battles but it was attacked by bands of mercenaries. In Upper Auvergne, the peasants revolted. This was the "Tuchins' War".

It was not until the end of the 15th century that the troubles died away and prosperity returned to the region with the expansion of the paper industry in Ambert and the cutlery industry in Thiers. Riom and Salers became affluent thanks to the presence of law courts while Saint-Flour's wealth came from trade. In the Velay area, there were a number of large, prosperous abbeys such as La Chaise-Dieu or Le Monastier.

The town of Ambert (Puy-de-Dôme).

After the flight of the Constable de Bourbon to the Court of Charles the Fifth, Holy Roman Emperor, the Bourbonnais was annexed to France.

The Wars of Religion in the second half of the 16th century left a trail of arson and slaughter right across Auvergne. The Protestants were in the minority but they had a stronghold in Issoire. The town remained in the hands of the famous Huguenot captain, Merle, for a short time before being recaptured by the Catholics. In Velay, the Abbey of La Chaise-Dieu was pillaged. Le Puy was one of the last Leaguer towns to recognise the authority of Henri IV.

After the Edict of Nantes, peace returned and the Protestants were granted a few churches, for example La Gazelle (Cantal), and Maringues (Puy-de-Dôme).

In the 17th century, Auvergne began to recover from its misfortunes. Yet it was often subjected to outbreaks of plague and to marauding bands of soldiers. It was also going through a period of economic stagnation.

Security, though, was gradually re-established with the development of the absolute monarchy. Richelieu had numerous castles razed to the ground and he rescinded the assembly of the "Good Towns of Auvergne". An extraordinary Court met in Clermont for the "Grand Days of Auvergne".

In the 18th century, royal Intendants did their best to improve the region's economy. One example was the attempt to improve cheese production by bringing in gruyere specialists from Switzerland.

Apart from the Reign of Terror, the French Revolution was often seen as no more than a sequence of events in Paris, news of which took many days to reach the region.

A few famous members of the Montagnard faction played a decisive role in the Revolution, e.g. Carrier, the M.P. for Cantal who drowned prisoners in the river at Nantes, and Couthon who came to Clermont-Ferrand on official business on several occasions.

Yet the most famous personality of this period was General Lafayette (1757-1834), who was born in Chavaniac in Haute-Loire. He was a hero of the American War of Independence and a key figure during the French Revolution.

The economy, which could hardly have been described as thriving when the monarchy was restored, was to undergo renewed expansion in the mid 19th century, thanks to the development of new transport systems. The Périgueux-Clermont-Lyons and Paris-Clermont-Aurillac roads date from this period. The Clermont railway

The famous Abbey of La Chaise Dieu (Haute-Loire).

was opened in 1856; Aurillac followed in 1868. Such major projects required a huge work force.

After the period of prosperity for vineyards (1850-1890), the population again began to emigrate. This movement away from the region became permanent, replacing the traditional, but temporary emigration of men from the Livradois district who used to head for the Atlantic ports where they worked as pit-sawyers, the canvas merchants from Le Cézallier, or even the people of Cantal who were to be found working as bakers in Barcelona as far back as the 16th century.

The rural exodus resulted, of course, in an aging population and an agricultural system that ground to a halt.

At the same time, Clermont benefitted from local, and later foreign immigration, supplying the work force for major industries.

The provincial capital of Auvergne, a large but soporific centre of trade in the latter years of the 19th century, became a dynamic regional capital which now lies at the junction of several motorways. This should improve its chances of fighting off the centralising influences which suggest that part of Cantal should look towards Toulouse, while part of Haute-Loire should centre on the Rhône-Alpes region.

In this lush, wooded region, man has left numerous traces of his existence, some of them grandiose, some more modest, but all of them a moving sight.

A predilection for Romanesque architecture

The region's architectural heritage, although widely-varying, is dominated by mediaeval buildings in the Romanesque and Gothic styles that developed differently as a result of varying sources of influence.

Visitors must, of course, see the main churches in Lower Auvergne, in which the proportions are particularly harmonious, churches in places such as Saint-Nectaire, Orcival, Saint-Saturnin, Issoire, or Notre-Dame-du-Port (in Clermont-Ferrand). All of them are similar for their chancel with ambulatory and apsidal chapels, and the Galilee porch preceding the nave.

The largest Romanesque church in Auvergne is to be found in Brioude (St. Julian's Basilica, an ornately-decorated and vividly-coloured church because of the many tints and hues in the building materials used).

But quite apart from these "major" monuments, Auvergne is filled with churches and chapels that integrate perfectly into their surroundings. Some stand high on a rock, staunchly overlooking a valley; other huddle in the depths of wild ravines. It is worthwhile getting off the beaten track to find them. A few examples would be, in Cantal, St. Madeleine's Chapel near Massiac; in Haute-Loire, Prades, Sainte-Marie-des-Chazes, or Chanteuges in the upper Allier region; Arlempdes and Chama-

The church in Sainte-Etienne-de-Vicq, to the north-east of Vichy (Allier).

The cloisters in Lavaudieu Abbey, 6 miles from Brioude (Haute-Loire)

The fresco depicting the "Liberal Arts" in the Relics Chapel in Le-Puy-en-Velay (Haute-Loire).

lières on the banks of the R.Loire, Le Monastier-sur-Gazelle and Saint-Front at the foot of Le Mézenc; and, in Puy-de-Dôme, the sanctuary in Dauzat-sur-Vodable in the "divided country".

Although the region retains an image of mainly Auvergnat Romanesque architecture, there are several major places of interest which have been subject to influence from horizons far and wide. Such is the case of Notre-Dame Cathedral and Saint-Michel-d'Aiguilhe in Le Puy-en-Velay, both of them masterpieces of Romanesque architecture of Byzantine inspiration.

The Gothic style, which is fairly uncommon in Auvergne, is nevertheless present in a few, outstan-

ding buildings e.g. the cathedral in Clermont-Ferrand, St. Lawrence's Church in Le-Puy-en-Velay, the abbey of La Chaise-Dieu, the chancel of the cathedral in Moulins, the cathedral in Saint-Flour and St. John's Church in Ambert.

The decorative features in this religious heritage are extremely elegant and varied. Particular attention was paid to the capitals, which blend perfectly into the architecture as a whole, whether they consist of foliage as in Orcival and Saint-Saturnin, or figures relating a story as in Issoire, Saint-Nectaire and Brioude, where the carvings relate themes from the Bible or Antiquity.

Auvergnat art and architecture also include other, highly original

creations such as statues of the Virgin Mary in Majesty ornamented with gold and silver (Orcival) or painted wooden statues of the Virgin (Museum of Religious Art in the cloisters in Le-Puy-en-Velay), crucifixes, reliquaries (Auzon), and superb busts (St. Baudime in Saint-Nectaire, St. Chaffre in Le Monastier-sur-Gazelle).

Murals and frescoes are also numerous, and of a quality rarely seen e.g. St. Michael the Archangel (12th century) in the cathedral in Le-Puy-en-Velay, Chasteloy-en-Bourbonnais (12th century), Saint-Julien-de-Brioude (13th century), the Assumption and Coronation of the Virgin Mary in Billom (14th century), Lavaudieu (14th century), *St. Georges killing the dra-*

gon in Ebreuil (15th century), the *Liberal Arts* (15th century) in Le-Puy-en-Velay, and the famous *Danse macabre* (15th century) in La Chaise-Dieu.

Finally, the Christian faith left its mark in the many stone or wrought-iron crosses set up at road junctions throughout Auvergne, where they bear witness to age-old beliefs.

A land of castles and eyries

As a region that was the object of immense jealousy for many years, Auvergne developed a whole network of fortresses which made optimum use of the lie of the land, from the Celtic hillforts of which the most famous is Gergovia, to the fortified strongholds of the Middle Ages.

Thereafter, the buildings took on a more human appearance. With the arrival of the Renaissance, architecture reflected the will to improve living conditions, leaving us a few charming residences ornamented with parks and gardens. The towns themselves were affected by this fashion and, from being previously austere fortresses, they became real urban centres, encouraging the development of the arts.

Nowadays, there are two tourist routes covering the places that are most representative of the region's history. The first of these is the Auvergne Castle Trail (*Route des Châteaux d'Auvergne*); the other is the Lafayette Road. The Castle Trail includes six routes through the Bourbonnais and Limagne regions, Volcano Country (*Pays des Volcans*), the uplands of Cantal, and the Livradois-Forez area, with some forty suggestions of places to visit. Among them,

Overleaf : Busséol Castle, near Vic-le-Comte (Puy-de-Dôme).

Below : a typical house in the uplands of Cantal.

The Coq Noir mountain hut in the Forez Mountains.

the most famous are Lapalisse, Toury, Billy, Effiat, Cordes, Murol, Tournoël, La Batisse, Val, Anjony Vollore, Ravel and Chavaniac-Lafayette.

The latter is also included in the Lafayette Road which runs along the upper reaches of the Loire, marking out a tourist trail with a cultural slant. Arlempdes, Goudet, La Tour-Daniel, Lavoute-Polignac, and Roche-Baron are dotted along the banks of the river, all of them major places of interest. Others include Valprivas, Chalencon, Saint-Vidal, La Rochelambert, and Polignac.

A number of Auvergne's towns are also worth a special mention because of the wealth of interesting buildings e.g. Riom, Montferrand, Clermont-Ferrand, Moulins, Cusset, Aurillac, Saint-Flour, Le-Puy-en-Velay, not forgetting Salers, Murat, Billom, Thiers, Blesle or Brioude.

As to the 19th century, it has left us such famous bridges as the Garabit Viaduct (designed by Gustave Eiffel in 1884), and the Fades Viaduct, while the Second Empire left its own particular style on the spa town of Vichy (Grand Casino).

Variety in rural housing

There is another, more modest type of architectural heritage which must be taken into account and which varies greatly depending on environmental and historical conditions. According to the lifestyle of their occupants, houses range from having flat tiled roofs in the north to rounded, "Roman" tiles in the south and the layout of the houses also changes depending on the altitude. In the Buron area of Cantal or in the farmhouses of the Mézenc, the houses are stocky buildings covered with thatch or flat stone slabs designed to withstand the rigours of the winter. At the other end of the scale are the traditional houses of Grande Limagne, a cereal-growing area in which the houses are built around a square courtyard decorated with a dovecot.

Building materials are varied, and ingenious, changing from one region to another. Houses may be built of lava, granite, or arkosic sandstone, or they may have walls of limestone or even wattle and daub in areas where there is little building stone available.

Auvergne is a region of plains, plateaus and mountains, and visitors are always surprised by the richness and variety of its landscapes. Around the heart of the region, in the Allier Vallier and the Limagne, the area has a high proportion of farmland stretching over four *départements*, i.e. Allier, Cantal, Haute-Loire and Puy-de-Dôme.

This area extends beyond the historical borders of Auvergne, which was limited approximately to Puy-de-Dôme, Cantal and the Brioude district.

It is a transitional region between northern and southern France. The typical features of housing from north to south, where flat tiles give way to rounded Italianate tiling, is a strong indication of this evolution.

In fact, the famous 45th parallel, which passes through the southern part of the region, the high level of sunshine (more than 2,000 hours per year in Haute-Loire), and the Occitan origin of the local dialect show that the region is, without any doubt, situated at the gateway to the south.

The Limagne

This is a vast, fairly varied plain which some have compared to the plain in Alsace. The rift valley is limited on the western edge by the scarp slopes marking the line of faults in the string of extinct volcanoes known as the "Puys", and to the east by the Forez uplands.

The area is subdivided into Grande Limagne stretching from Coudes to the confluence of the rivers Allier and Sioule, and Southern Limagne where the plains are smaller and the landscape of extinct volcanoes more rugged.

The plain is exceptionally fertile, indeed it is comparable to the Beauce. The Grande Limagne is a land of black earth which grows maize, sunflowers, corn or sugar beet. There is no longer any trace of the marshlands that are mentioned in Roman days. They were drained off to Pérignat-les-Sarliève and Saint-Ignat near Maringues.

The plain has adapted particularly well to extensive cereal farming.

The soil type, however, is not uniform across the entire region. It varies from marl in the plain to sand and clay in the wastelands. Particularly common in the Randan and Lezoux areas, they are easily spotted in the landscape dotting it with wooded areas and poorer soil. They then extend into the Sologne Bourbonnaise to the north of Varennes-sur-Allier.

Finally, the plain is dotted with limestone hills and rises to the north of Riom, while the uplands to the south are volcanic in origin. This area, which has become residential, had its moment of glory in the late 19th century when wine production was at its height. In 1885, the Puy-de-Dôme was the third largest wine producer in France. Nowadays, the Saint-Pourçain area has specialised in high-quality wines.

Scenery in Southern Cantal : the Aubrac area.

A valley in the heart of the Cantal Mountains.

In all, it is a sparkling, vivid region that is presented for your delight, framed by the mountains in the Puy ranges that bar the horizon.

The volcanic uplands of the west : the Monts d'Auvergne

Spread out in a north-south line through the *départements* of Puy-de-Dôme and Cantal, the volcanic uplands consist of five individual ranges i.e. the Puys or Monts Dôme, the Monts Dore, the Cézallier, Cantal and part of Aubrac.

Les Puys is a line of mountains extending over a distance of 29 miles from north to south, a few miles to the west of Clermont-Ferrand. Its main feature is the string of 80 eruptive volcanoes that are fairly young (they vary from 15,000 to 3,500 years B.P).

Over the past few years, the landscape in this area has undergone remarkable change. What were once moorlands filled with heather and broom have become more wooded as a result of both natural evolution and the action of the forestry commission since the days of the pilot scheme carried out by Count de Montlosier in Randanne, for it has to be said that the abandoning of sheep pasture leaves the way open for scrub, hazelnut trees and birches.

The Monts Dore are older and more complex. Their highest peak is the Puy de Sancy (alt. 6,126 ft) and they almost gave their name to the *département* known as Puy-de-Dôme. However, the Member of Parliament, Gaultier de Biauzat, preferred the name Puy-de-Dôme because it sounded less of a synonym for wealth and affluence ("or" means "gold").

This range of mountains is crisscrossed by rivers and streams and specialises in animal farming and the production of saint-nectaire cheese for which the area covered by the registered name of origin coincides almost exactly with the edge of the highland region. This is also the area for spa towns, with major centres such as La Bourboule, Le Mont-Dore and Saint-Nectaire.

The Monts du Cantal to the south consist of an extensive volcanic upland which, although rising to only 6,029 ft. at the Plomb de Cantal, is the largest range of volcanic mountains in Europe with a diameter of 43 miles, comparable to Mount Etna.

Equally distributed between two radiating valleys and extensive planezes, the hills specialise in animal farming. It is here that cantal cheese is produced, with saint-nectaire in the north. However, very few family cheese-making huts (called "*burons* ")still exist.

Unlike the other mountainous areas, the **Cézallier** and **Aubrac** regions are rather more reminiscent of upland plateaus. They both consist of basalt tables with an altitude of 3,900 ft. for Cézal-lier and between 4,225 and 4,550 ft. for Aubrac.

The eastern uplands

In the Western Velay, the volcanic uplands of **Le Devès** resemble those of the Puys, with conical mountains and large lava flows. Yet the lie of the land is less rugged.

The area is marked by the blunt-tipped mounds that are typical of this region, the "gardes" . Crops are grown to a level halfway up the hills, where Norway pines take over.

The Sancy range.

The Eastern Velay covers older volcanic uplands such as **Le Mézenc** and **Le Meygal**. Pelé-type cones (known locally as "sucs") stand high above the great planeze. Isolated phonoliths including Mont Meygal (4667 ft.) or more massive summits such as Le Mézenc, the highest mountain in Haute-Loire at 5697 ft., mark the landscape. From the promontories along the eastern edge of Auvergne, there is a magnificent view across the Alps in general and Mont Blanc in particular.

The crystalline plateaus of the west

The granite and gneiss base rises from north to south of Auvergne, with altitudes ranging from 975 ft. to 5200 ft.

The **fields and hedgerows of the Bourbonnais** are the heart of the *département*, lying between Allier and Cher, where the Côtes Matras stand high above lush meadows surrounded by hedges. The Queune Plateau and the limestone plateaus of Saint-Menoux and Souvigny are covered with fertile fields while from Bourbon-l'Archambault to the Cher Valley the region is full of forests, the delight of the Bourbonnais, Trançais, Gros-Bois, Dreuille and Civray areas. The rivers Oeil and Aumance drain a basin in which Charolais cattle are the major industry.

The area stretching from Montluçon in Allier to the edges of Mont Dore is called **Combrailles** and it is an area of fields, hedgerows and small farms. It remains a border between the nearby Limousin and the Limagne, an area that has enjoyed rather more success than its neighbour in stock-breeding and major agricultural output.

The **Artense**, to the south, stretches over the *départements* of Puy-de-Dôme and Cantal, from the edges of Monts Dore to the Dordogne Valley. This relatively low plateau still bears clear traces of glacial erosion, with undulating relief created by deposits of morainor erratics.

To the south of Cantal lies the **Châtaigneraie**, a sloping plateau with an altitude ranging from 2,600 ft. down to 1,300 ft., cut by deep valleys. It shows a strong southern French influence with its tall houses and countless fruit trees.

Forming the transitional belt between Cantal and Haute-Loire, the highest summit in **La Margeride**, a granite batholith to the west of Allier, is Mont Mouchet (alt. 4,550 ft.).

The crystalline plateaus of the east

The eastern mountains differ from their western counterparts

An aerial view of the Velay region.

The Montagne Bourbonnaise.

for the larger stretches of forest. The crystalline base has been dislocated and fractured here.

The **Montagne Bourbonnaise** is the highest and coldest area in Allier. It has an excellent water supply and, is therefore, lush and green, yet the crop yields are often mediocre. Its grassy slopes and beech or pine forests have led to its nickname, "Little Switzerland". Summer and winter tourism has provided the area with welcome additional income,

especially in La Loge-des-Gardes.

The region blends into Puy-de-Dôme through the **Bois Noirs** rising to 3,900 ft. and, more particularly, through the **Monts du Forez**. These mountains rise to 5,310 ft. at Pierre-sur-Haute, forming the frontier with the neighbouring *département* of Loire.

The numerous streams that gush down the western side of the mountain gave rise to a number of thriving businesses in the Middle

Ages. The alpine pastures still have their mountain farms where cheese used to be made, reminders of a rural life long gone.

Finally, between the Allier and Dore Valleys, are the **Monts du Livradois**, a less compact range rising to 3,932 ft. at the Signal de Mons.

To the south, the **Plateau de La Chaise-Dieu** forms a perfect peneplain at an altitude of 3,250 ft., in a region that grows a wide variety of crops.

ONE OF THE FINEST AREAS OF VOLCANIC UPLAND IN THE WORLD

The outstanding natural heritage formed by the **Chaîne des Puys** is classified as one of the world's major beauty spots. It is a veritable museum of volcanic shapes but there is no danger now on the slopes of the volcanoes; they are there for all to enjoy. Most of the mountains have retained a remarkably youthful shape thanks to their recent creation, and they can be seen and appreciated in their entirety by visitors, without any need to be an eminent expert in volcanoes.

The general public has a tendency to see volcanoes in terms of cones or domes, yet the structure of volcanoes is far from being as limited.

Most of the extinct volcanoes are of the Stromboli type and have common features such as the formation of a cone of volcanic slag, in some instance with lava flows at the base. The cone may be simple (Puy des Goules), breached (Puy de la Vache), or double-interlocked (Puy de Côme).

The Pelé-type volcanoes are fewer in number and are caused by an acid, viscous magma which accumulates at the time of eruption. The gases can only escape by means of terrible explosions,

The Puy de Dôme.

*The Puy de la Vache, at the southern end of
the volcanic mountain range.*

Another view of the Puy de Dôme.

causing much-feared clouds of burning matter. The lava from these volcanoes is lighter in colour and known as domite or trachyte. Volcanoes of this type in the Puy-de-Dôme include Le Sarcouy and Chopine.

The "maars" have little effect on the lie of the land. They correspond to craters formed by explosions when ground water came into contact with rising magma. The crater may be filled by a lake (Gour de Tazenat) or by marsh-land (Narse d'Espinasse), or it may be filled in. As research progresses, this type of volcanic structure is becoming increasingly frequent. The Place de Jaude in Clermont-Ferrand lies on the site of a crater that is 140,000 years old.

The landscape along the Puy ridge can be seen in its entirety from the summit of the Puy-de-Dôme.

Unlike the volcanoes in the Puy ridge, the **Monts du Cantal** constitute a strato-volcano, which corresponds to the heaping up of successive layers of ash, pumice, and breaches gashed by extrusions of viscous lava alternating with flows of more fluid lava.

This old volcano now seems to have been almost completely broken down by erosion. Glaciers reshaped the landscape. It is only from the Col de Serre or the summit of Puy Mary that you can really appreciate the beautiful bowl or cradle-shaped valleys that

23

Scenery in Northern Cantal.

radiate out from the summit (Impradine Valley, and the cwms in Mandailles and Le Falgoux).

Volcanic movements in Haute-Loire occurred from the Upper Miocene to the beginning of the Quaternary (the Villefranche Era). They are evident in the Hercynian structure that was broken and folded during the Tertiary Era. Volcanic terrain produces varying shapes combining cones of lava slag, with circular depressions caused by explosions, basalt tables, phonolithic outcrops or lifting in sedimentary basins.

The **Devès or Western Velay**, bordered by the Allier, Loire and Borne Valleys, consists of a crystalline horst with an altitude of approximately 3,250 ft. topped by Stromboli-type cones and draped in basalt flows. The Lac du Bouchet is a fine example of a maar.

The **Eastern Velay**, extended on the eastern edge by the **Mézenc, Meygal and Vivarais**, consists of a heaping up of basalt flows but includes a few maars (Saint-Front). Above it rise remarkable volcanoes of the Pelé type.

The **Puy-en-Velay Basin** at the confluence of the rivers Borne and Loire is famous for its picturesque scenery. It includes the Corneille or Saint-Michel rocks consisting of breaches dating from the Villefranche Era and the open series of soft sediment that surround them, forming necks. The freshness of the outlines is also evident and symbolised in the columnar basalt at Espaly.

L'Emblaves, which lies beyond the Oligocene sinkhole of Le-Puy-en-Velay, is separated from it by the horst of Chaspinhac which is also dotted with outcrops of rock that indicate the presence of viscous lava (Ceneuil and Courniol, alt. 2,564 ft. and 2,454 respectively).

Nowadays, everybody is attentive to the quality and power of water. And in this respect, Auvergne enjoys inestimable wealth in the form of thousands of miles of clear waters, hundreds of mineral springs, and dozens of volcanic lakes, all making this a privileged and well-preserved region. The water table runs down to the Dordogne on one side and the rivers Allier and Loire on the other. The main river in Auvergne is the Allier, which crosses the region from one end to the other, after rising in Le Moure de la Gardille in Lozère. Great tributaries such as the Sioule and Alagnon on the left bank and the Dore on the right swell its waters until, at the Allier Bill, it joins the royal river, the Loire. This regal waterway rises at the foot of the Mont Gerbier-de-Jonc in Ardèche and flows through admirable gorges and a wide, winsome valley as it crosses the *département* of Haute-Loire, the "land of the Young Loire". The river and its tributaries have very irregular flows. The wrath of these capricious waterways is well-known and has led to the building of constructions that are designed to tame some of their impetuosity. The policy of river improvement has now resulted in the controversial dam project at Serre de la Fare, upstream from Le-Puy-en-Velay.

With the river, of course, go the bridges. Brives-Charensac (which gets its name from Brivas, a Celtic place name meaning "bridge") dates from the mid 12th century; Coubon was rebuilt after

The upper reaches of the R. Loire running through a gorge.

The R. Sioule seen from Le Château Rocher between Ebreuil and Châteauneuf-les-Bains.

the 1980 flood and is crossed in the middle by the famous 45th parallel. The bridge at Moulins was rebuilt fifteen times between the 15th and 17th centuries. The rivers were, for many years, a means of communication used to transport raw materials up and downstream. Jumeaux and Pont-du-Château acquired their affluence from this river traffic. The water was also the basis of industries such as cutlery making in Thiers and paper in Ambert, thanks to hydro-electric power. As to the mineral waters, they are bottled - can there be anybody who has never heard of Volvic or Vichy? Other less famous springs are also exploited e.g. Châteauneuf, or Sainte-Marguerite. These thermal springs, which were known in Roman times, have led to the creation of many spa towns, and Auvergne leads the way in hydrotherapy treatment in France.

Among the best-known in Allier are Bourbon-l'Archambault (rheumatism), Néris-les-Bains (nervous disorders), Vichy (disorders of the digestive system). In Cantal, there is Chaudes-Aigues whose spring water reaches a temperature of 82° C. And Puy-de-Dôme has La Bourboule (respiratory disorders), Chatelguyon (intestines), Le Mont-Dore (asthma) and Royat-Chamalières (arterial disease).

Nowadays, though, water is also synonymous with leisure and relaxation. Its quality is such in this region that it provides all types of fishing, e.g. trout, char, and Allier salmon. The latter has its own "Centre" in Brioude, where an aquarium that is the only one of its kind in Europe (containing 30 tonnes of water) enables visitors to follow the course of a "salmon river". Flat-rate angling permits and wild wa-

A fisherman in the R. Loire.

Overleaf : swimmers in Lake Chambon.

ter sports are on offer to enthusiasts, and the variety of rivers enables each to enjoy the leisure activity that he or she prefers. The Allier is as suitable for canoeing as it is, in its upper reaches, for rafting and hydrospeed. Numerous lakes or stretches of water are suitable for sailing, boating or swimming.

Although the people of Auvergne, Bourbonnais and Velay are proud by nature, they welcome tourists as friends and are always delighted to show their know-how and share their enthusiasm and taste for art and entertainment. Traditions are alive and well in Auvergne, like the cutlery industry in Thiers, lace-making in Le-Puy-en-Velay, or paper in Ambert. Yet the image of the locals was also praised by Georges Brassens who immortalised their generosity in song and, if Auvergne is not merely one large cheeseboard, it is, nevertheless, an area in which the art of good food is constantly in evidence. The variety of landscapes, the abundance of water, and the widely-differing terrains make it possible to enjoy all that nature can provide, and man has added his energy and ingenuity to these other, encouraging factors. The result in Auvergne is a well-garnished table and a reputation based on pork meat products, trout or salmon, mushrooms, lentils, and last but by no means least cheese (saint-nectaire, Cantal and Ambert fourmes, goats cheese from Le Velay etc.) and forest fruits. Auvergne's wines (Saint-Pourçain, Chanturgue etc.) and liqueurs (verbena (*Verveine*) from Le Velay etc.) complete the picture, and they are all used to their very best advantage by a generation of young chefs, most of whom belong to the "Toques d'Auvergne" association.

Tourists can also steep themselves in local customs, through visits to museums or through a number of special events. Several dozen museums retrace local his-

The Apple Festival in Ludesse (Puy-de-Dôme).

A basket of penny buns.

tory. There is, for example, the Cutlery Centre (*Maison des Couteliers*) in Thiers, the Richard-de-Bas mill in Ambert, the Headdress Museum (*musée de la coiffe*) in Blesle, the Perrel Brothers' Farm in Moudeyres, the Resistance Museum in Mont-Mouchet, the La Margeride Folk Museum in Loubaresse, and the Tin Museum (*musée du Fer-Blanc*) in Saint-Arcons. Lace-making is both presented as a museum piece and taught in Le-Puy-en-Velay and Brioude. As to the Volcano Park (*Parc des Volcans*), it has several centres open to visitors, veritable regional showcases in their own right. There is the Stone Centre (*Maison de la Pierre*) in Volvic, the Volcanism Centre in Montlosier, the Cheese Centre (*Maison des Fromages*) in Egliseneuve-d'Entraigues, the Water and Fishery

Rural self-catering in Le Claux (Cantal).

Centre (*Maison de l'Eau et de la Pêche*) in Besse, the Gentian Centre in Riom-ès-Montagnes, the Shepherd's Hut (*Buronnier*) in Laveissière near Super-Loiran, the Wildlife Centre (*Maison de la Faune*) in Murat, and the Peat Centre (*Maison des Tourbières*) in Saint-Alyres-ès-Montagnes. But most of all, visitors should not leave the area without having visited the museums that have particularly rich collections of exhibits such as the Bargoin and Ranquet Museums in Clermont-Ferrand, the Regional Auvergne Museum and the Francisque Mandet Museum in Riom, the Upper Auvergne Museum in Saint-Flour, and the Crozatier Museum in Le-Puy-en-Velay.

Finally, the local people do their utmost every year to bring alive for visitors the main events in the history of Auvergne. In authentic settings, they stage pageants designed to take you back in time. In Murol Castle, for example, the Compagnons de Gabriel stage the life of the castle owners and peasants in the Middle Ages. In Salers, there is a day marking the Vow taken by the town. In Saint-Julien-Chapteuil and Pradelles, there are events illustrating the most intense periods in the history of the Velay area, while in the upper town in Le-Puy-en-Velay, there is an archery contest during the Festival of the Bird King which celebrates the opulence of the Renaissance during a week-long event.

In fact, most of the year is marked out by major events. "General Winter" is burnt during the fantastic carnival in Le-Puy-en-Velay, flooding the streets of the town with "bandas" and costumed participants. Spring is also celebrated in carnivals in Yssingeaux, St Didier en Velay, Ygrande and Vichy. Street theatre is the order of the day in Aurillac, during a European festival that is held in high esteem. Tauves holds the Laquais Drama Festival. Most of the cinema news is to be found in Clermont-Ferrand, during the Short Film Festival. Folklore has gained acceptance in Gannat and Le Velay, as have puppet shows in Le Mayet-de-Montagne or Ambert, the town beloved of Jules Romains for his unusual meeting there with "the mates". Literary academies also show the intellectual brilliance of the region, especially the Bourbonnais. As for poetry, it brings enlightened ama-

Hacking the Haute-Loire, in the volcanic uplands of Le Mézenc.

teurs to the upper Allier every year as summer draws to a close.

The Street Festival in Aurillac (Cantal).

Above all, though, it is music which is highlighted in Auvergne, in particular at the prestigious, and internationally-famous, Festival de la Chaise-Dieu. This festival draws thousands of music lovers to the abbey every year at the end of August and beginning of September and plays a major role in establishing the image of Auvergne and Haute-Loire as regions with particular cultural value. In the same way, the Auvergne Regional Orchestra acts as an ambassador for its region. This love of music can be seen in the calendar of concerts i.e. Bourbonnais Music Festival, Summer Music in Vichy, concerts in Vollore or Aulteribe, Piano Festival in Riom, Musical Evenings in Chazeron, Music Festivals in Thiers or Pionsat, International Festival and Academy of Brass Bands in Monastier-sur-Gazeille, Music and Dance Festival in Le-Puy-en-Velay-Saint-Vidal, and concert seasons in Valprivas.

Cultural events are, then, many and varied in Auvergne and, when you add to this extensive selection, the outdoor leisure activities such as rambling, pony trekking, cycling, fishing or wild water sports and the many discovery trails (Cheese, Lace-making, Auvergne castles, Lafayette etc.), it is easy to understand Auvergne's attraction for visitors. And this description would not be complete without a mention of the quality of the air and the crystalline light, both of which are much appreciated by hang-gliders or those who enjoy parapente (on the Puys range or Mézenc), gliding (Issoire, Loudes) or aeronautical thrills. The pilots meet in Haute-Loire every year for the weekend of 11th November where they create a wonderful show full of magical colours.

Allier

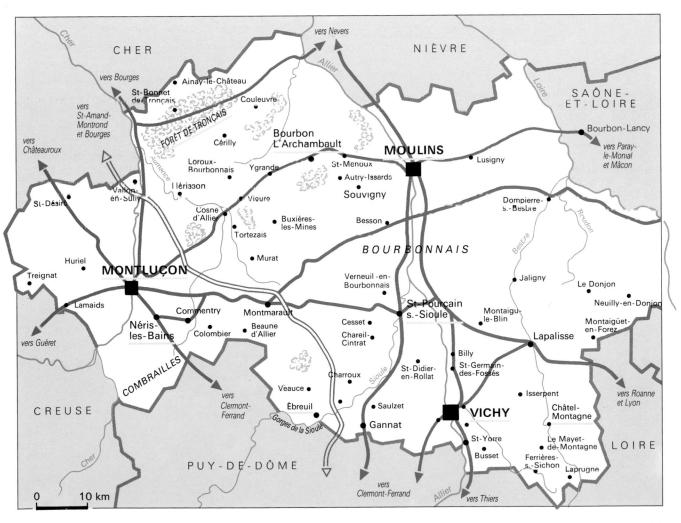

vers Nevers

CHER
NIÈVRE
SAÔNE-
ET-LOIRE

vers Bourges

Ainay-le-Château
St-Bonnet
de-Tronçais
Couleuvre

vers
St-Amand-
Montrond
et Bourges

FORÊT DE TRONÇAIS

Bourbon-Lancy

vers Paray-
le-Monial
et Mâcon

vers
Châteauroux

Cérilly
Bourbon
L'Archambault

MOULINS

Lusigny

Loroux-
Bourbonnais
Ygrande
St-Menoux

Hérisson

Autry-Issards
Souvigny
Dompierre-
s.-Besbre

St-Désiré
Vieure
Cosne
d'Allier
Besson

Vallon-
en-Sully
Buxières-
les-Mines
Tortezais

Huriel
Murat
BOURBONNAIS
Jaligny
Le Donjon

Treignat
MONTLUÇON
Verneuil-en-
Bourbonnais
Neuilly-en-Donjon

Lamaids
St-Pourçain
s.-Sioule
Montaigu-
le-Blin
Montaiguët-
en-Forez

Commentry
Montmarault
Cesset
Lapalisse

Néris-
les-Bains
Colombier
Beaune
d'Allier
Chareil-
Cintrat
Billy
St-Germain-
des-Fossés

vers Guéret

COMBRAILLES
Charroux
St-Didier-
en-Rollat
vers Roanne
et Lyon

Veauce
Isserpent
Châtel-
Montagne

CREUSE
Ébreuil
Saulzet
VICHY
Le Mayet-
de-Montagne
LOIRE

vers
Clermont-
Ferrand
Gorges de la Sioule
Gannat
St-Yorre
Ferrières-
s.-Sichon

PUY-DE-DÔME
Busset
Laprugne

vers
Clermont-Ferrand
Allier
vers Thiers

0   10 km

AINAY-LE-CHATEAU

Old fortified gateway. Skilfully-restored church containing a font thought to be an old Roman basin. Fine Renaissance doorway.

AUMANCE

River flowing through an attractive valley on the edge of the Tronçais Forest.

AUTRY-ISSARDS

Situated between Bourbon-l'Archambault and Souvigny. The chancel in the church houses a painting of Christ being taken down from the Cross (Flemish school, late 15th century). The Château du Plessis, which is visible from the road, is attractive and typical of 15th-century military architecture (not open to the public).

BEAUNE-D'ALLIER

The waters of St. Aignant's Fountain were said to cure eye diseases. When the level drops in Rivalais Lake, huge blocks of stone become visible, probably the remains of a Roman road.

BESSON

The "insane stone" or "yoke stone" is said to be an old dolmen. There are four listed castles viz. Vieux Bostz (15th and 16th centuries), Ristz (14th and 15th centuries), Rochefort (14th and 15th centuries) and Fourchaud (14th century). Empress Zita of Austria visited the modern Château de Bostz on several occasions.

BILLY

Extensive ruins of a 13th- and 14th-century fortress.

BIOZAT

Situated to the south-west of Vichy in the Limagne area. Delightful Romanesque church.

Fourchaud Castle in Besson : the rectangular keep dates from the 14th century.

Billy Castle.

Overleaf : Busset Castle near Saint-Yorre.

BOURBON-L'ARCHAMBAULT

This is the *Aquis Bormonis* on Peutinger's map, the town that gave its name to the longest-ruling dynasty of kings of France. The town includes the impressive ruins of the castle that provides the setting for *Flammenca*, a 13th-century poem expressing jealousy. This is a spa town, with a number of famous visitors to its credit (Mme de Montespan, Charles-Maurice de Talley-rand-Périgord). The museum houses a fine collection of pharmacists' jars, and the statues of Our Lady of Vernouillet and St. Grelichon. In the nearby Gros-Bois Forest are the ruins of Grammont Abbey and an old statue of St. Fiacre, the patron saint of gardeners.

BUSSET

Castle with foundations dating back to the 13th century. 16th-century gallery with mid 16th-century murals based on the poems of Henri Baude. Residence of the Bourbon-Bussets, whose eldest son is currently a member of the Académie Française.

CERILLY

A small town to the north-east of Montluçon, not far from the Tronçais Forest. 12th-century church. Unusual statue depicting

A stucco statue of the Laying in the Tomb in the church in Cérilly. It dates from 1691. The figures, including the kneeling donor, are all life-sized.

Christ being laid in the tomb (17th century). Birthplaces of several famous men e.g. Marcelin-Desboutin, engraver, Jacques Chevalier, philosopher, Marcel Héraud, former Cabinet minister, Jean Giraudoux and Charles-Louis Philippe, writers. On the square is a bust of François Péron, who travelled through the southern hemisphere.

CESSET

Sights include the Chenillat keep and the Château de Valbois in which Valéry Larbaud rested and Roger Caillois, a member of the Académie Française, lived for some time.

CHANTELLE

Situated to the north-west of Vichy. Ruins of an 11th-century fortress. The cloisters in this fortress, which was Anne de Bourbon's favourite residence and from which Charles III, Constable of France, set off to lead a revolt against King François I, are occupied by Benedictines, who sell an excellent eau de cologne. Conventual church. Sightseeing in the vicinity includes the Château de la Croisette (Renaissance), and Etroussat (church with fourteen modern stained glass windows by a master glass painter named Duran).

CHAREIL-CINTRAT

16th-century castle with decorative features that are risqué, not to say licentious. Château du Bas-de-Chareil (fine murals in shades of brown depicting themes from mythology and astrology).

Above : the remains of the castle in Chantelle.

Opposite : the tympanum on the Romanesque church in Bellenaves, between Chantelle and Ebreuil.

CHARROUX

Picturesque old village to the north-west of Vichy, with houses dating from the 15th to 17th centuries. Interesting museum currently being extended. 12th-century church.

39

The church in Chatel-Montagne.

CHASTELOY

12th-century church overlooking the Aumance Valley. Frescoes date from the 13th to 17th centuries. For the past twenty years, a music festival has been held here every summer with five concerts given by famous orchestras and internationally-famous artistes.

CHATEL-MONTAGNE

A village in the Montagne Bourbonnaise, to the east of Vichy and south of Lapalisse. The 12th-century church is one of the finest examples of the Auvergne Romanesque style in the region. It is said to have been built originally by Melusinette the Fairy. Good centre from which to visit Puy du Roc (alt. 2,093 ft.). Magnificent view.

COLOMBIER

A village to the south-east of Montluçon. Celtic fountain with three basins. 11th-century church with multifoiled doorway.

COMMENTRY

Town to the south-east of Montluçon. Thanks to the coal beneath it, it became an industrial centre but the recent economic crisis has necessitated change. A number of famous people lived in the town e.g. Emile Mâle, member of the Académie Française, the novelist and journalist Marcelle Auclair, the novelist Henri Laville, the painter Aujames and, of course, Christophe Thivrier, known as "Cristou", a member of parliament who was always dressed in overalls. In more recent times, the town has been home to the singer, Henri Tachan.

CUSSET

A town adjacent to Vichy. It was here that King Charles VII was reconciled with his son, the future King Louis XI.

DESERTINES

This locality is better-known as "La Biache", a name which originated from the term "ouche", a word with a German origin, or from "bignache", a local dialect word for the basket in which workmen used to keep their packed lunch. In the church, which was skilfully restored in 1974, there is a statue of St. George on horseback and a magnificent modern copper statue of Christ made by Jacky Pinon.

DOMPIERRE-SUR-BESBRE

A small town in the delightful Besbre Valley (excellent fishing) to the north-east of Vichy. Sightseeing in the vicinity should include Sept-Fons Abbey (3 miles

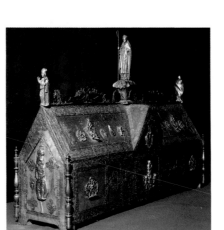

Top to bottom : Château de Toury-Ebreuil near Dompierre-sur-Besbre; the knocker on the church door; St. Léger's reliquary.

Overleaf : Chouvigny Castle to the west of Ebreuil.

away), Puy Saint-Ambroise (panoramic view), the castles of Beauvoir (13th century) and Toury, the village of Saligny-sur-Roudon, and Le Pal Zoo.

EBREUIL

A large village to the west of Vichy. Charles the Simple owned a villa here. St. Léger's Church dates from the 10th and 13th centuries (12th-century porch-belltower, 12th and 15th-century frescoes, magnificent 16th-century reliquary of St. Leger). This is a very attractive area (Colettes Forest) much frequented by artists. To the west is Chouvigny Castle (13th century, restored in the 20th century) and the Chouvigny Gorge. Superb scenery.

FERRIERE-SUR-SICHON

A very attractive region that is popular with tourists, in the Montagne Bourbonnaise. Fairy Grotto. Nearby is St. Vincent's Rock (wonderful panoramic view). Montgilbert Castle was once the home of the famous adventurer, Rodrigue de Villandrando and is said to contain a hidden treasure. There is an Archaeology Museum in Glozel.

GANNAT

A town to the west of Vichy. The feudal castle was used as a prison before becoming the Museum of the Occitan Gateway Treasures. The museum houses the saddlery, the cars owned by the Barons of Veauce, and the 9th- and 10th-century "Book of Gospels". Gannat is the setting for a World Folklore Festival, held every year at the end of July.

HERISSON

A village in the Aumance Valley to the north-east of Montluçon. Ruins of a 13th-century castle. Wonderful view. Village once lived in by the painter Harpignies (1819-1916).

HURIEL

Situated to the west of Montluçon. Square keep (nicknamed "the chef's hat") that was once part of the 12th-century castle. Old wine-growers' houses. Old wine presses.

Top to bottom :
- St. Vincent Rock near Ferrière-sur-Sichon, where Christianity and paganism become inextricably entwined;
- the town of Gannat.

Opposite : Hérisson Castle.

ISSERPENT

The "Dancing Stone" is of Celtic origin.

JENZAT

A village to the west of Vichy. 11th-century church. Wonderful frescoes by the "Masters of Jenzat", depicting Christ's Passion and the martyrdom of St. Catherine.

LAMAIDS

Once a commandery of the Knights of St. John of Malta. The church has recently been restored. Note the beautiful modern stained glass by Jacky Pinon.

LAPALISSE

A town to the north-east of Vichy on the banks of the R.Besbre. Superb castle built in the 12th century with central section dating from the 16th century. It was commissioned by Jacques II de Chabannes, Lord of La Palice, Maréchal of France. He died at Pavie. After his death, his soldiers wrote a song which went like this, "Monsieur de la Palice is dead, He died before Pavie, Alas were he not already dead, He'd arouse very great envy". Later, the last line was changed to "He would alive still be", which has given rise to an French word "lapalissade" meaning "truism". The body of the brave Maréchal, who did not deserve to be made fun of in a popular song, was brought back to France and buried in a marble tomb that was destroyed during the French Revolution by troops from Marseilles on their way to Paris. The castle is worth a visit. In the vicinity, note the Château du Vieux-Chambord (13th, 14th, and 16th centuries), the Parc des Gouttes (leisure complex, animals) and the village of Jaligny where the novelist René Fallet wrote his finest works.

LAPRUGNE

Situated to the south-east of Vichy in the Montagne Bourbonnaise area. St. Mary Magdalen Priory. The "Daytime Stone" (*pierre du jour*) is worth a look. Numerous so-called "Druid" stones. Winter sports centre with ski slopes in La Loge-des-Gardes. Several local

Château de Lapalisse.

Château de Jaligny, in the Besbre Valley.

villages are worth a visit e.g. La-voine (an ethnic group known as the "Supervisors" (*Pions*) has left a legend of strong resistance to pro-gress), and Saint-Priest-la-Prugne in the Bois Noirs (sawmills).

LE VERNET

The town lies on the outskirts of Vichy. It is a cultural centre and the seat of the Le Vernet Aca-demy which has awarded an an-nual literary prize for the past for-ty years. The prizewinners range from Barjavel to J. de Bourbon-Busset, from Jeanne Cressanges to J. Pelletier Doisy and Ginette Briant, and from René Fallet to Pierre Miquel, a list that would be worthy of the better-known Gon-court Prize. Every year, the Aca-demy organises art exhibitions with guest visitors such as Car-zou, Hilaire, Jansen, Michel Ciry, Buffet, etc. on behalf of Vichy town council.

During the fourth Biennial Fes-tival of writers from the Bourbon-nais region, which was held in the Senate thanks to the good offices of Jean Cluzel, there was an exhi-bition of the 140 works from the Bourbonnais area published over the previous two years.

LOUROUX-BOURBONNAIS

Situated on the GC 16 road. There are three other villages called Louroux i.e. Louroux-de-Beaune, Louroux-de-Bouble where the church contains works by Pierre Lafoucrière, and Louroux-Hode-mont on the GC 39. In the Mont es-tate, there is a magnificent menhir.

47

LUSIGNY

Eight miles east of Moulins. The Château de Pomay was purchased by the wife of Surintendent Fouquet who was then under house arrest in Montluçon. In May and June 1676, she received a visit from the Marquise de Sévigné.

MAYET-DE-MONTAGNE

Main town in the Montagne Bourbonnaise area to the southeast of Vichy in the Sichon Valley. See the basin stones in Courtine and the foot of the Wandering Jew. Lunar sanctuary dedicated to Belisama and sacrificial altar stones.

MEAULNE

A small community to the north of Montluçon, in the Aumance Valley, which gave its name to the title of a famous novel, *Le Grand Meaulnes*, by Alain-Fournier whose parents were primary

Above : Near Le Mayet-de-Montagne.

Below : The castle of the Dukes of Bourbon stands high above the town in Montluçon.

teachers 4 miles from here, in Epineuil-le-Fleuriel.

MONTAIGU-LE-BLIN

Situated to the north of Vichy. 13th-century castle said to have been the birthplace of Maréchal de La Palice.

MONTLUCON

Economic capital of the Bourbonnais area, in the heart of the Upper Cher Valley. The town lies beneath the walls of the only Bourbon castle still standing. It dates from the days of the One Hundred Years' War and now houses the Folk Museum and the International Hurdy-Gurdy Museum. Below the castle is the Old Montluçon Centre. Also worth a visit are Notre-Dame Church (15th century) and St. Peter's Church (*église Saint-Pierre*) dating from the 12th and 13th centuries, the Boris-Vian Centre, the Federates Theatre and the Athanor Cultural Centre. Montluçon was the birthplace of André Messager who composed operettas such as *Véronique*, of Achille Allier, and of Jean and Marx Dormoy. A variety of pear, the *"sucrée vert de Montluçon"*, makes the town's name well-known in fruit-growing circles.

Huriel Church, near Montluçon.

MONTMARAULT

Since the opening of the A71 motorway, this has become a major road junction.

MONTOLDRE

Situated between Montaigne-le-Blin and Saint-Pourçain to the north of Vichy. Gayette Castle has a 15th-century keep; it has become a home for the elderly mentally handicapped. René Fallet used

the village as the setting for one of his novels, *Les Vieux de la Vieille*.

MOULINS

Capital of the Bourbonnais region, on the banks of the R. Allier. 15th-century houses. Notre-Dame Cathedral. The former collegiate church, which has magnificent stained glass windows, dates from the 15th century; the towers and

nave are 19th century. Note also the Black Virgin Chapel (13th century) and the famous triptych by the Maître de Moulins. Other sights in the town include the Jack-o-the-clock (belfry), the chapel in the Banville High School which contains the mausoleum of Duke de Montmorency, the statue of the poet Théodore de Banville (on the Square de la Gare), the "Mophead" (the keep of the Bourbons' castle), the Folk Museum and Mu-

seum of Old Moulins, the Art Gallery and Museum of Archaeology (in the Pavillon Anne-de-Beaujeu) and the Bourbonnais Local History Museum (in Yzeure). Nine miles to the north of Moulins is the Château de Riau (15th to 17th centuries) and, a couple of miles further on, the Balaine arboretum, a unique park well-stocked with botanic specimens.

MURAT

Situated to the east of Montluçon in the rural area of the Bourbonnais, in the Aumance Valley. Ruins of a large feudal castle. In the sacristy of the church, there is a 16th-century silver reliquary made to hold a piece of the True Cross and a Holy Thorn gifted by St. Louis to his son, Robert de Clermont, Lord of Bourbon.

Left : Moulins seen from the R. Allier with the cathedral and Sacré-Coeur Church in the background.

Below : the Jack-o'the-Clock in Moulins, taken from a narrow street.

The Black Virgin Chapel in Moulins Cathedral.

NERIS-LES-BAINS

A popular spa town 5 miles to the south-east of Montluçon known for its curative effects since the early days of Antiquity. The Rieckotter Museum has several interesting exhibits e.g. the goddess Epona, the god with the torque, Romanesque capitals etc. Near the church is a Merovingian burial ground. The town also has an arena and ancient baths. Néris-les-Bains is linked to Montluçon by a ramblers' path.

51

The tympanum on the church in Neuilly-en-Donjon.

NEUILLY-EN-DONJON

The tympanum is very famous. It was the first time that a Romanesque sculptor had carved a Madonna and Child on a church doorway.

SAINT-BONNET-DE-ROCHEFORT

A village near Ebrueil, to the west of Vichy. The foundations of the castle are thought to date back to the early 12th century. The castle contains magnificent 14th-century tapestries illustrating, among other things, Charles VI's insanity and Anne of Brittany's marriage.

The castle in Saint-Bonnet-de-Rochefort.

Another view of the castle in Saint-Bonnet-de-Rochefort.

Hence the nickname given to the coffin, the "*debredinoire*". In order to regain their common sense, all sufferers had to do was to put their head inside the coffin.

SAINT-POURCAIN-SUR-SIOULE

An administrative centre 17 miles north-west of Vichy. Birthplace of the theologian, Durand de Saint-Pourçain. Capital of Bourbonnais wines. See the Wine Centre where you can taste the sparkling "Anne-de-Bourbon". Also old Holy Cross Abbey (*abbaye Sainte-Croix*), 11th to 15th centuries.

SAINT-YORRE

A small town to the south-west of Vichy. The local mineral water was made famous in the 19th century by Nicolas Larbaud, chemist and grandfather of the writer, Valery Larbaud, whose mother called herself Larbaud Saint-Yorre.

SAULCET

A small village near Saint-Pourçain. Delightful church (frescoes dating from the 12th, 13th and 14th centuries). In the cemetery, covered over with ivy, is the grave of the Fauvist painter, Louis Neillot.

SAINTE-DESIRE

Impressive Romanesque church with crypt. St. Agatha's Chapel. Numerous traces of Stone Age settlements in Les Jayettes, the Four-Parchat Cave, the Dancing Stone etc.

SAINT-DIDIER-EN-ROLLAT

The chapter house of the abbey founded in 1152 by St. Gilbert is worth a visit. It has been skilfully restored and is now used an an exhibition centre for works by artists or craftsmen.

SAINT-MENOUX

A village almost 3 miles to the west of Moulins. 12th-century church. Archaeology Museum. The chancel of the church houses the stone coffin containing the mortal remains of St. Menoux, who had a reputation for curing the simple-minded, or "*bredins*".

SOUVIGNY

A small town to the west of Moulins with an eventful history. Magnificent priory (St. Peter's), dating from the 11th to 19th centuries : tombs of the Bourbon family, relic cabinets, cloisters and chapter house. Church, archaeology museum, 12th-century calendar.

A lake in the Tronçais Forest.

TORTEZAIS

Château de La Brosse-Raquin, the property of the descendents of Baron de Fain, Private Secretary to Napoleon I.

TRONCAIS FOREST

One of the most beautiful areas in Allier (in the north of the *département*). The forest consists mainly of common oaks with beeches and hornbeam below. In 1670, Colbert drafted the famous order to which we owe the wonderful oaks we see today (some of them are three hundred years old, reaching heights of up to 120 ft. with circumferences of almost 13 ft.). Lily of the valley, mushrooms, riding to hounds, way-marked forest footpaths, lay-bys, campsites and swimming in the lakes, make this a paradise for tourists. Especially worth a visit are the Priot, Saint-Bonnet and Saloup lakes, the Colbert woodland, and the Stebbing oak.

VALLON-EN-SULLY

A rural holiday location to the north of Montluçon, famous for its restaurants. Château du Creux : a fine 18th-century building containing an exquisite staircase built of local red sandstone.

VEAUCE

A small village 4 miles to the north of Ebreuil and the west of Vichy. A cultural venue popular with tourists. 11th-century Romanesque church, 9th-century fortress that was restored or extended from the 13th to 19th centuries. Every year an art exhibition and literary events draw a large number of visitors.

VERNEUIL-EN-BOURBONNAIS

A tiny village 4 miles to the north of Saint-Pourçain that has retained its mediaeval character. The local people organise exhibitions and high-quality literary events there every year.

LE VEURDRE

A village in the north of the *département*, on the banks of the R. Allier. Château de Saint-Augustin. Magnificent zoo.

VICHY

An attractive town, famous for its waters since the earliest days of Antiquity. Fortified town during the Middle Ages. Seat of the French government during the Second World War. A number of illustrious visitors have come to take the waters here e.g. the Marquise de Sévigné, Louis XV's daughters, Napoleon Bonaparte's mother, Napoleon III, numerous artists and politicians. Vichy offers visitors and tourists a very wide range of leisure activities and entertainments. It has top-quality sports amenities, especially for boating, and luxury shops. Sightseeing should include the

Top : the dome of the top-quality pump room in Vichy.

Bottom : the Célestins spring.

Above : Allier Lake in Vichy.

Opposite : near Bezenet in the Montluçon area.

Spring Park (parc des Sources) and the Allier Park, St. Blaise' Church, the Missionary Centre (Maison des Missions), Madame de Sévigné's house, the sweet factory (2 miles from town) in which the famous Pastilles Vichy are made, Les Hurlevents (a beauty spot 3 miles from town) from which there is a fine panoramic view, and the small spa of Bellerive (1 mile from town).

VIEURE

Château de la Salle and the ruins of the Château de la Chaussière which once belonged to Anne of Bourbon. The sacristy in the church houses a famous painting entitled "St. Luke painting the Virgin Mary" by Colyn de Coter.

YGRANDE

A small town to the south-west of Bourbon-l'Archambault. 12th-century church. Emile-Guillaumin Museum, named after the farmer-writer, the author of "La Vie d'un Simple". Every year, since time immemorial, the carnival has been an opportunity for enjoyment. It is attended by people from all the neighbouring départements.

YZEURE

On the outskirts to the east of Moulins is Font-Saint-Georges, which was honoured by the poet Théodore de Banville. Bourbonnais Local History Museum.

56

Cantal

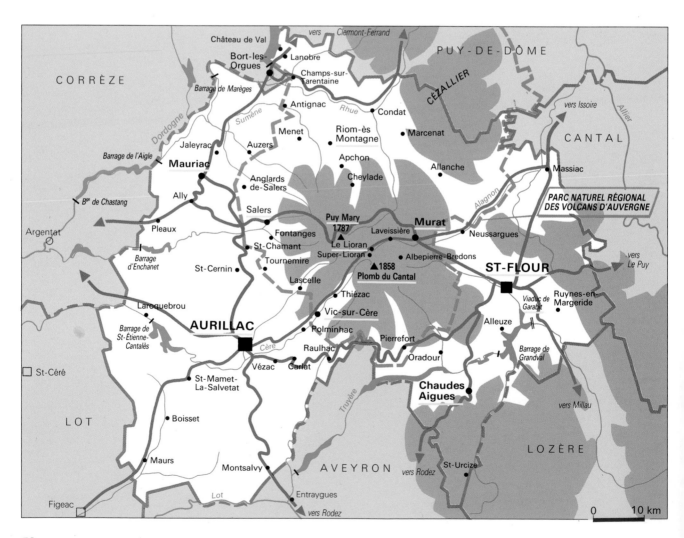

Château de Val
Bort-les-Orgues
Lanobre
Champs-sur-Tarentaine
vers Clermont-Ferrand
PUY-DE-DÔME
CÉZALLIER

CORRÈZE
Barrage de Marèges
Antignac
Rhue
Condat
vers Issoire

Sumène
Menet
Riom-ès-Montagne
Marcenat
CANTAL

Dordogne
Jaleyrac
Auzers
Apchon
Allanche
Massiac

Barrage de l'Aigle
Mauriac
Anglards-de-Salers
Cheylade
Alagnon

B⁰⁰ de Chastang
Ally
Salers
Puy Mary 1787
Laveissière
Murat
Neussargues
PARC NATUREL RÉGIONAL DES VOLCANS D'AUVERGNE

Argentat
Pleaux
Fontanges
Le Lioran
Super-Lioran
Albepierre-Bredons
ST-FLOUR
vers Le Puy

Barrage d'Enchanet
St-Chamant
Tournemire
1858
Plomb du Cantal

St-Cernin
Lascelle
Viaduc de Garabit
Ruynes-en-Margeride

Laroquebrou
Thiézac
Alleuze

Barrage de St-Étienne-Cantalès
AURILLAC
Cère
Vic-sur-Cère
Polminhac
Pierrefort
Barrage de Grandval

St-Céré
Vézac
Carlat
Raulhac
Oradour

St-Mamet-La-Salvetat
Chaudes Aigues
vers Millau

LOT
Boisset

Maurs
LOZÈRE

Montsalvy
St-Urcize

Figeac
Entraygues
AVEYRON
vers Rodez

Lot
Truyère
vers Rodez

0   10 km

ALLANCHE

Allanche, in the heart of the Cézallier area of Cantal, remains the largest town in the upper plateaus. It grew up around a priory which depended upon the Abbey of La Chaise-Dieu.

The Romanesque church (12th century) has three aisles, an apse and three apsidal chapels. In the 14th century, after disorders that were caused by the One Hundred Years' War, fortifications were added to the building (watchtower).

There are two small chapels in Maillargues and Chastres.

Allanche Fair.

Lac du Pécher near Allanche.

Not far away is the Lac du Pécher and the Pinatelle Forest where you might hear the baying of a stag.

ALBEPIERRE-BREDONS

Situated on its neck of basalt, the church in Bredons (11th-12th centuries) stands high above the town of Murat and overlooks the Alagnon Valley. The spot was once the site of a Cluniac priory. The timber-roofed nave is flanked by side aisles with semi-barrel vaulting. Three gilded wooden reredos cover the wall in the apse.

ALLEUZE

Situated in a grandiose, wild stretch of countryside, the Château d'Alleuze juts out above the skyline at the top of a peninsula. It consists of a square keep flanked by four round towers, now in ruins.

A Romanesque church (12th century), which underwent extensive modification in the 15th century, has some delightful moulding round the doorway dating from the late Middle Ages.

ALLY

The town has both interesting remains of the Early Middle Ages and the **Château de la Vigne** (late 15th century) which was built for the Scorailles family. The chateau still has its 16th- and 17th-century murals and, in the chapel, you can see angels bearing the instruments of Christ's Passion. The Chamber of Justice contains portraits set amidst arabesques.

The chateau has several buildings and towers, topped by parapet walkways over machicolations.

During the summer months, it hosts a Miniature Car Exhibition.

ANGLARS-DE-SALERS

The **Château de la Trémolière** (late 15th century) has a superb collection of Aubusson tapestries, some of which date back to 1586. They depict real or imaginary animals on a background of greenery and architecture. The chateau is open to the public during the summer.

The village has a delightful Romanesque church with a particularly admirable chevet and apse.

ANTIGNAC

Above the Sumène Valley at Le Roc Vignonet are the ruins of a church that was once dependent on the priory of La Chaise-Dieu.

The Consuls' Residence in Aurillac.

60

The Carmelite Gardens in Aurillac.

The Sumène Valley Historical and Archaeological Research Group has opened a popular ethno-botanic garden presenting plants grown in the past.

As to the site of the mediaeval quarry at Les Roussillous, it is to be turned into an Archaeology and Ethnology Centre specialising in rural life during the Middle Ages, with a particular interest in plants and woodlands in every period of history.

APCHON

Little is left of the castle that once belonged to the powerful Lords of Apchon whose influence spread far beyond the bounds of Cantal. Nowadays, only a few ruins jut up from an outcrop of basalt.

The tiny church contains a magnificent wooden reredos carved in the 16th century.

AURILLAC

Aurillac, which lies in the heart of the basin in a decidedly rural setting, already has a Southern-French charm despite being situated not far from Cantal's largest volcano.

There are several buildings worth a visit e.g. St. Géraud's Church which, until the French Revolution, belonged to a large Benedictine abbey founded by Count Géraud in 916 A.D. Inside, the chapel of Our Lady of the Chancel (*Notre-Dame-du-Choeur*) contains an 18th-century altar. The Church of Our Lady of the Snows (*Notre-Dame-des-Neiges*) was part of a Franciscan friary which was demolished during the French Revolution. Built in the Southern French Gothic style, it still has a fine chapter house.

There are a number of museums and exhibition centres open to the public, among them the J-B Rames Museum of Arts and Popular Traditions, the H-de-Parrieu Museum (paintings, sculptures,

AUZERS

Auzers Castle (14th-15th centuries) has a central section flanked by towers and a ring of machicolations at roof level. Frescoes dating from the 16th century decorate an old shrine (open to the public in the summer months).

BRAGEAC

Above the Auze Gorge cutting deep into the old crystalline shelf is the church of the former Benedictine abbey, a Romanesque building with a triple-spanned central nave. The bases and capitals of the pillars are well-preserved. They show a variety of designs, especially animals and foliage.

CARLAT

Carlat has given its name to the Carladès region, a landscape broken up by valleys and basalt tables. It is on one of these plateaus that the feudal fortress of Carlat was built, but little trace remains of it today. The fortress,

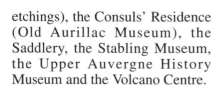

Above and opposite : the fountain on the Place Saint-Géraud and the old theatre door.

Below : a thatched cottage in the Carladès region.

etchings), the Consuls' Residence (Old Aurillac Museum), the Saddlery, the Stabling Museum, the Upper Auvergne History Museum and the Volcano Centre.

The Carladès region near Carlat.

which was apparently an impressive sight, was demolished on the orders of Henri IV.

The Gothic style church has a 17th-century reredos behind the High Altar.

CHAMPS-SUR-TARENTAINE

In the north of Cantal in the heart of the Artense area lies Champs-sur-Tarentaine, close to the confluence of the rivers Rhue and Tarentaine.

Lastioulles Lakes has been equiped for sailing and provides a range of water sports.

CHAUDES-AIGUES

This small spa owes its reputation to its hot springs, which have been famous since the beginnings of the Christian era. They reach a temperature of 82°C.

The town has an impressive Gothic church containing a 19th-century altar screen carved by a local artist.

CHEYLADE

Cheylade, situated in one of the valleys that radiate out from the Puy Mary, has a church that is remarkable for the decoration of the ceiling in the nave. Each coffer in the wood panelling has been decorated with flowers, fruits, or animals representing Noah's Ark, as well as the coats-of-arms of the region's families. In all, 1360 panels were painted in this way during the 18th century.

Not far away is the village of Le Claux. It was no more than an offshoot of Cheylade until 1835 but has now become a dynamic holiday centre in its own right.

From here, you can climb up to the Limon Plateau, a vast area of summer pasturage. On the plateau are numerous ruins showing the

Cheylade Church.

existence of erstwhile human habitation. In the 12th century, Cistercian monks set up an agricultural community named "La Grange de Gaule" (*The Barn of Gaul*). The farm was abandoned after the One Hundred Years' War.

FONTANGES

Fontanges, on the banks of the R. Aspre, not far from Salers, remains a particularly delightful Cantal village, with a few houses that bear witness to the prosperity of earlier years. It gave its name to Marie-Angélique de Fontanges, one of Louis XIV's favourites.

The church has a nave flanked by seven chapels, ending in a three-sided apse. There are a number of admirable altar screens in the side chapels. The door opens onto the south, beneath a porch with ribbed vaulting.

The Château de Palmont in the Maronne Valley was a fortified 15th-century manorhouse to which a wing of private apartments was added in the 19th century.

JALEYRAC

The Romanesque church with the single aisle is important for its large set of 15th-century frescoes depicting scenes of martyrdom (decapitation, St. Agatha having her breasts ripped off, St. Martin sharing his cloak etc.)

LANOBRE

Lanobre lies a few miles from Bort-les-Orgues (Corrèze) in Artense. It has several buldings and museums that are worth a visit.

First of all, it has a Romanesque church with very high-quality archi-

Lanobre : the door of the Romanesque church.

The Château de Val in Lanobre.

tecture, containing some attractive capitals and carved modillions. The doors are skilfully decorated with wrought ironwork.

The **Château de Val** (15th century), which is silhouetted against the lake formed by the Bort-les-Orgues Dam, remains a fine specimen of military architecture. It houses top-quality painting or crafts exhibitions during much of the year.

Finally, the **Radio and Phonograph Museum** offers visitors a chance to discover the history of radio from its beginnings until the Second World War. It contains unsuspected treasures that enthusiasts have lovingly collected and brought together here.

LAROQUEBROU

Laroquebrou at the mouth of the Cère Gorge is in a wonderful setting at the gateway to the South of France.

The 14th-century Gothic style church has a four-span nave flanked by eight side chapels. Note the carved modillions and gargoyles.

Above : the lake at Saint-Etienne-Cantalès near Laroquebrou.

A few miles away is the Saint-Etienne-Cantales Lake, a 560-hectare stretch of water that offers a wide range of sports and leisure activities.

LASCELLE

In Lascelle, at the end of the Jordanne Valley, is St. Rémy's Church, a superb Romanesque building whose origins date back to a priory that was dependent upon St. Géraud's Abbey in Aurillac. It contains frescoes in the north chapels (Last Judgement, Christ on the Cross) and a rich collection of furnishings (polychrome wood, statues, reredos).

LAVEISSIERE

The most popular tourist attraction in Laveissière, not far from Super-Lioran, is the Volcano Park Centre, the **Shepherd's House**. And indeed, the Belles-Aygues shepherd's hut contains a mock-up of the production of Cantal cheese in a hut on a summer pasture.

Super-Lioran has become the largest downhill ski resort in the Massif Central but visitors can also enjoy cross-country skiing in the nordic area of Haute-Planèze. Summer visitors will be able to admire some exceptionally fine views of the surrounding summits from Font-d'Alagnon or Font-de-Cère.

MASSIAC

The town was built in a picturesque setting between two outcrops of basalt to either side of the R. Alagnon. One of these rocks is topped by the Chapel of St. Mary Magdelene, a small Romanesque church with frescoes painted between the 12th and 14th centuries.

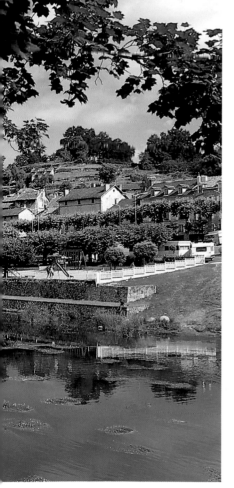

Opposite : Laroquebrou, a delightful setting.

Below : The Belles-Aygues cheese-making hut in Laveissière.

The other, the Plateau Saint-Victor, is a defensive site which has been occupied since the Stone Age. On it are the remains of a village that was abandoned in the 17th century.

MAURIAC

Mauriac, to the north-west of Cantal, looks as if its origins go back many years. In Gallo-Roman times, Mauriac was already a large *vicus*, as shown by the many remains that have been unearthed here.

In the old monastery, which was left abandoned for many years, restoration work has revealed the Romanesque chapter house, and the foundations of the chancel for St. Peter's Church.

With Notre-Dame-des-Miracles, Mauriac has the largest and arguably the most beautiful Romanesque church in Upper Auvergne. It has a nave with five spans, beneath a ribbed barrel vaulted roof. The chancel consists of a straight span and a semi-circular apse. The carved doorway in the West Front is magnificent, with its tympanum depicting two angels to either side of Christ in Glory. On the lintel are the Virgin Mary and the twelve Apostles.

The old "good town of Upper Auvergne" has an interesting architectural heritage, especially in the Orcet Residence, now the sub-prefecture offices.

MAURS

Maurs opens onto the South of France, forming a transition between south-west Cantal, the Quercy and the Rouergue. The town, which grew up around a Benedic-

The tympanum on Mauriac church.

tine monastery, still has an old minster (14th-15th centuries) in which the most important item is a reliquary bust of St. Césaire. It is of Romanesque origin and closely resembles the statue of Sainte-Foy-de-Conques.

MENET

Menet in the heart of the Artense area of Cantal has a Romanesque church with remarkable capitals in the nave and side aisles.

The Puy de Menoire is still topped by an early mediaeval fortress which is well-preserved.

MURAT

Flanked by the Bredons and Bonnevie Rocks, the former sub-prefecture has kept all its charm, with its beautiful stone-roofed houses (in particular, the old Consuls' Residence). The late 15th-century church contains a

A carved Crucifix near the church in Dienne, not far from Murat.

Montsalvy : a house on the Chataigneraie Plateau.

Overleaf :
- top, the admirable panoramic view of the Mandailles Valley at Le Puy Mary;
- bottom, the town of Murat.

statue of Our Lady of the Olive Trees which was said to have been brought back from the Holy Land by a knight.

The **Wild Life Centre** introduces visitors to animals in their natural setting, and contains several remarkable collections.

ORADOUR

Rochebrune Castle (13th and 15th centuries) in Oradour contains a range of magnificent collections (paintings, glass).

PIERREFORT

Pierrefort lies on the south-facing slopes of the Cantal uplands and remains a lively little town. Sightseeing in the vicinity should include the 13th-century

Boyle Castle high above the Brezons Valley, and Turlande Rock and Chapel which stand on the plateau.

From 16th to 20th August, the town stages a festival of popular arts and traditions, with a mock Auvergnat wedding and a giant Aligot.

Finally, there is one strange event that is worth mentioning - the square bowls competition.

POLMINHAC

Situated just a few miles from Aurillac, Pominhac is dominated by Pesteils Castle whose magnificent square keep dates from the 15th century. The main apartments were added in the 17th century. The keep contains superb frescoes depicting heroes of Antiquity e.g. Julius Caesar, Pompei etc.

LE PUY MARY

Although this is not the highest peak in Cantal (alt. 5,808 ft.), it is nevertheless the point of convergence of a number of radiating valleys e.g. the Santoire Valley leading to Dienne, the Impradine Valley leading to Lavigerie, the Rhue Valley (Cheylade), the Mars Valley (Le Falgoux), and the Aspre, Bertrande and Jordanne Valleys (Mandailles). In fine weather, the view stretches from the Sancy Range to the mountains of

Above : The Puy Mary, south face.

Opposite : The Puy Griou.

Below : Roland's Breach.

Margeride and Aubrac and beyond to the Lot Valley and plateaus of Corrèze.

Tours of the Mandailles Cwm are organised during the summer months.

RAULHAC

Occupied since the Stone Age, as proven by the latest digs in Ventecul, Raulhac has two inter-

The Puy Mary : the Impradine Cwm.

esting buildings viz. the church which was rebuilt in the late 15th century and the Château de Messilhac overlooking the Goul Valley. It is one of the few examples of Renaissance architecture in this region. The main building and entrance are very richly decorated and are flanked by two side towers dating from an earlier period (14th century).

RIOM-ES-MONTAGNES

Riom-ès-Montagnes is a small industrial town and business centre in the heart of northern Cantal. Its church, St. George's, is a Romanesque building rebuilt in the late 11th century and consisting of a triple-spanned nave and side aisle with interesting carved decorations (door jambs in the nave and capitals in the chancel).

The Volcano Centre has set up the **Gentian and Medicinal Herb Centre** in Riom. It offers visitors a chance to see an audio-visual presentation and an exhibition relating to plants. Its most popular feature is its superb botanic garden.

Scenery in the Margeride area.

RUYNES-EN-MARGERIDE

The Margeride, a transitional region situated between Cantal and Haute-Loire, contains nume-rous places of interest in a geographical setting in which many of the peaks near 5,000 ft.

The **Margeride Folk Museum** offers visitors a chance to see the Peasant's House and Forge, the Schoolhouse in Signalauze, the Longevialle Estate and the Ruynes Tower. Taken as a whole, the museum is very successful.

The town of Saint-Flour.

The Garabit Viaduct.

SAINT-CHAMANT

The castle keep is topped with battlements and dates from the 15th century. It houses a collection of Aubusson tapestries.

The fairly modern church (19th century) has an admirable set of carvings and paintings on wood on the choirstalls of the former collegiate church.

SAINT-FLOUR

Clinging to a basalt scarp slope, the town of Saint-Flour blends perfectly into a remarkable setting high above the rivers Ander and Lescure. It has been the seat of a bishopric since 1317 and is the religious capital of Upper Auvergne. The cathedral, on which building work started in the 15th century,

The Margeride Meetings (*Rencontres de Margeride*) attract large numbers of visitors during the first week of August, for a series of cultural events.

Not far away, the Garabit Viaduct built in 1882-1884 by an engineer named Boyer, to plans drawn by Eiffel, rises to a height of 397 ft. for a length of 611 yds.

was very badly damaged during the French Revolution but was restored in the 19th century. The most admirable features are the simple nave, the portraits of diocesan bishops, a 17th-century lectern and a fine statue of Christ. There are also some remarkable frescoes in the porch, in the North Tower and in St. Vincent's Church, especially in the second and third north chapels.

The town also has a number of particularly worthwhile museums e.g. the Upper Auvergne Museum in the former 17th-century Bishop's Palace which contains archaeological collections and exhibits relating to popular arts and traditions, the A-Douet Museum in the former Consuls' Residence with its art collections, and the Post Office Museum which spe-

Alleuze Castle to the south of Saint-Flour.

The Place Tyssandier-d'Escous in Salers.

cialises rather more in the history of the Post Office and in Garabit.

SALERS

One of the most delightful towns in Upper Auvergne and a sight not to be missed. The town, laid out on a basalt plateau high above the Maronne Valley, owed its prosperity to the Montagnes balliage in 1564. Numerous houses with stone-slabbed roofs on the Place Tyssandier-d'Escous or in the Rue des Nobles are examples of the high quality of the local architecture.

The church, which was rebuilt in the 16th century, was consecrated in 1552. It includes a single nave with ribbed vaulting onto which open six side chapels. At the end of the nave is a five-sided chevet. The church contains a superb statue of the Laying in the Tomb dating from 1496, an attractive Louis XIII lectern and two paintings attributed to Ribera.

The Knights Templars' House, a wonderful Renaissance mansion, has been turned into a Museum of Arts and Traditions. It has exhibits relating to the Salers breed of cattle and the manufacturing of Cantal cheese.

The Bargues Residence (15th century) is also open to the public.

THIEZAC

The small town of Thiézac in the Cère Valley has a Gothic church containing a 17th-century reredos and a statue of Christ being Scourged dating from the 16th century. To the north of the town lies the chapel of Notre-Dame-de-la-Consolation, which contains a reredos made in 1663 and a painted ceiling depicting flowers, fruit and subjects illustrating the litanies of the Virgin Mary.

Not far away is the entrance to the Castelniet Rocks, a rockfall caused by the collapse of one side of the valley.

TOURNEMIRE

This small village has one of the finest castles in the region, Anjony. It consists of a single keep flanked by four towers and is an excellent example of 15th-century military architecture in Cantal. Inside is a remarkable set

The small village of Thiézac in the Cère Valley.

of frescoes, in the chapel and the Knights' Hall.

VIC-SUR-CERE

Vic, in the upper Cère Valley, has existed since Roman times. It was once the judicial capital of the Carladès. This small spa town, where the climate is particularly healthy, has a Romanesque church built in the 15th century; the modillions of its chevet are especially interesting. The **Château de Comblat**, part of which dates from the 18th century, was a school for many years.

YDES

Situated in the north of Cantal, this small town has a remarkable church built during the second half of the 12th century by the Knights Templars and altered in later years. The carvings in the building, especially in the porch, show the Annunciation and Daniel being saved by Habbakuk in the lions' den. The modillions in the apse, the capitals and the bases of the pillars were produced by a very high-quality workshop.

A Butterfly Museum has a collection of strange insects, scorpions and butterflies.

Ydes : a close-up of the church.

Haute-Loire

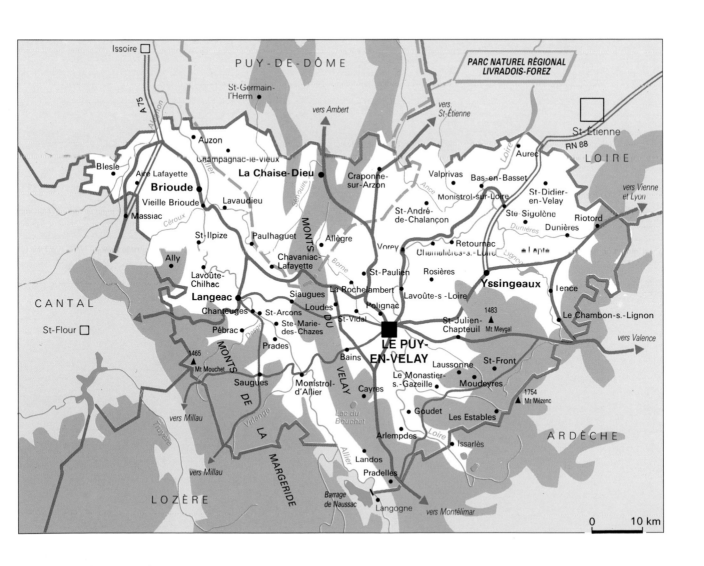

Issoire ☐

PUY-DE-DÔME

PARC NATUREL RÉGIONAL
LIVRADOIS-FOREZ

St-Germain-
l'Herm

vers Ambert

vers
St-Étienne

St-Étienne ☐

A 75

Auzon

RN 88

LOIRE

Blesle

Champagnac-le-vieux

Aurec

Aire Lafayette

La Chaise-Dieu

Craponne-
sur-Arzon

Valprivas

Bas-en-Basset

vers Vienne
et Lyon

Brioude

Monistrol-sur-Loire

St-Didier-
en-Velay

Vieille Brioude

Lavaudieu

Céroux

St-André-
de-Chalançon

Ste-Sigolène

Dunières

Riotord

Massiac

Ally

St-Ilpize

Paulhaguet

Allègre

Vorey

Retournac

Chamalières-s.-Loire

Lapte

Chavaniac-
Lafayette

Borne

St-Paulien

Rosières

Lavoûte-
Chilhac

La Rochelambert

Lavoûte-s -Loire

Yssingeaux

Ience

CANTAL

Langeac

Siaugues

Polignac

1483

Le Chambon-s.-Lignon

Chanteuges

St-Arcons

Loudes

St-Julien-
Chapteuil

Mt Meygal

St-Flour ☐

Pébrac

Ste-Marie-
des-Chazes

St-Vidal

LE PUY-
EN-VELAY

vers Valence

Prades

Bains

Laussonne

St-Front

1465

Mt Mouchet

Sauges

Monistrol-
d'Allier

Cayres

Le Monastier-
s.-Gazeille

Moudeyres

MONTS

DE

Arlempdes

Goudet

Les Estables

1754

Mt Mézenc

ARDÈCHE

LA

vers Millau

Vinlango

Lac du
Bouchet

Loire

Issarlès

MARGERIDE

vers Millau

Allier

Landos

Pradelles

LOZÈRE

Barrage
de Naussac

Langogne

vers Montélimar

0   10 km

ALLEGRE

Situated at the foot of Mont Bar (alt. 3,802 ft.), a Stromboli-type volcano, the village is dominated by the famous "gibbet", the remains of a 14th-century castle. Also worth a visit is the fortified Clock Gate known as "Monsieur". There is a wonderful view of the scenery in the Velay and Forez and across the Cévennes.

Arlempdes : the ruins of the old Montlaur Castle.

ALLY

This town, on the edge of Haute-Loire and Cantal, is famous for its old windmills (some of them have been restored) and a 19th-century antimony mine.

ARLEMPDES

The fortified ruins of the old Montlaur Castle (12th-15th centuries) stand high above the hillside village of Arlempdes in the wild gorges of the Loire. It includes a Romanesque chapel (11th and 12th centuries). Diane de Poitiers, Henri II's mistress, was Lady of Arlempdes in the16th century. In 1783, one of the descendents of the Arlandes family accompanied Pilâtre de Rozier during the first hot air balloon flight. Nearby are the picturesque villages of Salettes and Lafarre, on the banks of the upper reaches of the royal waterway.

AUREC

This bustling town in the low-lying Loire Valley boasts the world's leading manufacturer of swords, supplier to many a national fencing team and a number of prestigious military academies. Water sports complex and leisure amenities.

AUZON

A mediaeval town, once one of the "Thirteen Good Towns" of Auvergne. Auzon lies in the shadow of the Collegiate Church of St. Lawrence, a 12th-century sanctuary which contains several works of art, in particular a Romanesque wooden Crucifix and a late 15th-century statue of the Virgin Mary.

A wooden Crucifix in Auzon church.

gnat Romanesque styles, its museum filled with treasures of religious art, the Dukes of Mercoeur Tower also known as the "Twenty Angles" Tower, a 12th-century keep, and the narrow winding streets of half-timbered houses dating from the 14th and 15th centuries or houses with turrets dating from the 16th century.

BRIOUDE

Brioude, a bustling sub-prefecture with a population of 8,000, lies on a terrace overlooking the fertile Allier Plain. Its geographical situation provides it with an excellent dry, temperate climate, and pure invigorating air.

The town is famous for salmon-fishing. The best period extends over the months of February, March and April when the fish swim upstream from the ocean to spawn in the cold waters of the upper reaches of the Allier.

Brioude developed in the Gallo-Roman period. The martyrdom of St. Julian in the early years of the 4th century turned it into a much-frequented place of pilgrimage throughout the Middle Ages.

From the 9th century to the days of the French Revolution, the town lived under the temporal and spiritual authority of a chapter of Chanoine-Comte. The main building of interest in the town is St. Julien's Basilica, the large Romanesque church in Auvergne.

The earliest foundations date back to the 4th century, when they covered St. Julian's tomb. This

BAS-EN-BASSET

Bas-en-Basset is a charming little town on the banks of the R. Loire, and was once one of the largest harbours of the upper reaches of the river. The sunny climate is particularly favourable for water sports. The ruins of Rochebaron Castle (13th-15th centuries) include the remains of fortifications.

BLESLE

This large village full of mediaeval architecture is one of the "one hundred most attractive villages in France". Its history is closely linked to that of its Benedictine convent (9th century) which joined the Order of Cluny in 1628 and was closed during the French Revolution. Places to visit include St. Peter's Church (*église Saint-Pierre*) built in the purest of Auver-

The town of Brioude and St. Julian's Basilica.

early building was destroyed and rebuilt on several occasions. The church we see today dates mainly from the 11th and 12th centuries, although several major alterations were undertaken in the 13th and 14th centuries.

The use of different-coloured stone (grey, red, and black) set out in a uniform layout makes the building look like a mosaic.

The church is built to a simple design. The long nave (240 ft.) is preceded by a narthex (a Galilee, or external, porch). This porch is topped by a gallery with, above it, the square belltower on the West Front. Originally roofed with barrel vaulting, the nave was raised in the 14th century and given ribbed vaulting. The chancel is surrounded by an ambulatory opening onto five semi-circular apsidal (or radiating) chapels. A two-storey octagonal belltower rises above the transept crossing before the apse.

Attributed to several different workshops, the capitals in the nave and narthex are remarkable. They consist of foliage or figures and illustrate a number of themes that were dear to Romanesque symbolism. Early 13th-century frescoes were discovered c. 1960 in St. Michael's Chapel above the narthex. Other paintings can be seen on the first pillars in the nave and beneath the vaulted roof.

The basilica also contains several major works of art viz.

- Christ the Leper, a remounted polychrome wooden statue dating from the 15th century, which was brought here from the former leper hospital in La Bageasse;
- a reredos attributed to Vaneau (17th century) in the Holy Cross Chapel;
- a statue of the Virgin Mary in childbed;
- the High Altar in the chancel (17th century).

The town of Brioude is also worth a visit for its streets of old houses e.g. Rue d'Assas, Rue Séguret, Rue du 4-Septembre, or Rue de la Chèvrerie.

Other places of interest include the Lace Centre and the Salmon Centre, both of which only recently opened their doors to the public.

CAYRES-LAC DU BOUCHET

This is the main town of the volcanic Velay District. It has a fine Gothic church built of red tuft with a belltower that forms a turreted gable wall. Nearby is the Lac du Bouchet, a natural lake formed in a crater (45 hectares, altitude 3,926 ft.), which provides a haven of freshness and tranquillity within a pine forest, an ideal place for swimming, sailing, rambling and hacking.

CHAMALIERES

Situated at the end of a sheltered valley bathed by the waters of the R.Loire, Chamalières owes to its attractive geographical setting the installation of a Benedictine priory here in the 10th century, a daughter house of the Saint-Chaffre-du-Monastier Abbey. The church is without doubt one of the most remarkable buildings in the Velay region.

Le Bouchet Lake near Cayres.

Above : Chamalières-sur-Loire.

Below : A bas-relief in Chamalières church.

CHANTEUGES

Built on the slopes of a basalt flow separating the rivers Desges and Allier, the village is dominated by the old abbey built on the platform of the rock. With its small cloisters, the priory was once the summer residence of the Abbots of La Chaise-Dieu.

The interior of the church, which is lit by a large16th-century stained glass window, has some fine Renaissance choirstalls. There is a wonderful panoramic view of the Allier Valley.

Château de Chavaniac-Lafayette, where La Fayette was born in 1757.

CHAVANIAC-LAFAYETTE

Home of General Marquis de La Fayette (1757-1834), hero of the American War of Independence and a key figure during the French Revolution. The chateau, filled with period furniture (La Fayette's birthplace, guardroom, drawing rooms etc.) and memorabilia, is open to the public. There is also a waxworks museum illustrating the main events in the life of Gilbert Motier de La Fayette. Park, gardens, superb rose garden.

CRAPONNE-SUR-ARZON

Situated on the edges of the Velay region, Loire and Puy-de-Dôme, Craponne is a small but busy town which once supplied point lace to kings and queens, in the days when hand-made lace brought fame to the locality.

Of its feudal past, Craponne has retained a 12th-century quadrangular keep, and the remains of ramparts and fortified gateways. The 15th-century church contains an admirable alabaster statue of the Virgin Mary. There are also a number of 18th-century townhouses in a locality which celebrated its 1,000 years' history in 1990.

GOUDET

In an enchanting setting, in the shadow of the ruins of the old Beaufort Castle, Goudet is an ideal place to rest and relax on the banks of the young Loire and wild gorges, a paradise for trout fishermen.

LA CHAISE-DIEU

Situated in the depths of the Livradois Forest at an altitude of 3516 ft., La Chaise-Dieu is a rural holiday centre where the air is invigorating and ideal for those who enjoy outdoor activities.

Its Benedictine abbey was founded in 1043 by Robert de Turlande. In 1353, Pope Clement VI was buried here (tomb in the nave); it was he who commissioned the building of the present Gothic minster. In 1786, Cardinal de Rohan was exiled to La Chaise-Dieu after the "Queen's Necklace" affair.

The most interesting features are the famous fresco illustrating a *Danse macabre* (15th century), the 16th-century Flemish tapestries depicting scenes from the Old and New Testaments, the 144 carved choirstalls, the Echo Chamber etc.

Every year since 1966, at the end of the summer, this has been the setting for a prestigious music festival which attracts thousands of music-lovers, thereby contributing to the international fame of an entire region.

Close-ups of the "Danse macabre" fresco in the Abbey of La Chaise-Dieu. Death and the Lady, Death and the Minstrel.

Overleaf : A concert by the Moscow Philharmonic Orchestra in La Chaise-Dieu.

La Valette Dam.

LANGEAC

Langeac, a busy lively town in the heart of the Allier Valley which enjoys a particularly attractive climate, is an ideal holiday centre from which to tour all the sights and beauty spots in the region. St. Gall's Collegiate Church (15th century) has an elegant traceried belltower and contains fine 16th-century choirstalls.

LAPTE

Situated near La Vallette Dam (water sports complex), Lapte is best-known for its Neo-Gothic church (19th century) whose 175-foot belltower provides a vast panoramic view over the entire Yssingelais area.

LAVAUDIEU

Lavaudieu, the "Valley of God", which lies some six miles to the south-east of Brioude, has the remains of an old Benedictine convent created in the 11th century by St. Robert, the founder of La Chaise-Dieu. The church has an octagonal tower and contains some remarkable frescoes showing Italian influence (14th century). They represent figures such as Gabriel, the Virgin Mary or the Evangelists, alternating with story scenes such as Christ's Passion, the Dormition of the Virgin Mary, the martyrdom of St. Andrew, and an allegory of the Black Death (the plague that devastated mediaeval society).

Topped by a wooden gallery, the cloisters, which are the only ones left intact in Auvergne, have arcades over simple or double colonnettes rising to capitals that are fairly roughly carved.

The great refectory is decorated with a vast fresco illustrating Christ surrounded by the symbols of the four evangelists, and a Virgin Mary in Majesty flanked by adoring angels and the twelve Apostles.

Also worth a visit is the Haute-

Lavaudieu : the church cloisters.

impressive sight with the elliptically-fronted priory that was rebuilt in the 18th century. The treasure house contains a large 12th-century Crucifix, a wonderful wooden door (11th century) from the old church and the statue of Our Lady the Foundling, a small statue of the Virgin Mary (less than 1 inch high) which was discovered on the banks of the R. Allier in the 11th century and which has since been the subject of a famous pilgrimage.

LAVOUTE-SUR-LOIRE

The Chateau de Lavoûte-Polignac is, in fact, the first veritable Loire Valley castle, enclosed within a meander (or *volta*) of the royal waterway for more than one thousand years.

It was a country seat of the Polignac family and this proud building on which play the sparkling reflections of the young Loire, contains numerous objects linked to the History of France (in particular letters from Marie-Antoinette addressed to Duchess Yolande, her faithful friend).

A tour of this elegant castle gives some idea of the evolution of the Velay region over a period spanning more than ten centuries. The castle, which was first mentioned in the 9th century, was extended in the 11th, 13th and 14th centuries, partly demolished during the French Revolution and, finally, restored in the latter years of the 19th century.

LE CHAMBON-SUR-LIGNON

Le Chambon-sur-Lignon is a regional tourist centre catering for all types of sport and is an ideal, and well-known, rural holiday centre popular with those who

Loire Museum of Popular Arts and Traditions.

LAVOUTE-CHILHAC

Situated on a long, narrow tongue of rock that forces the Allier into a curve, Lavoûte-Chilhac is built on both banks of the river and is linked by an 11th-century stone bridge which was restored in the 15th century. Odilon de Mercoeur founded a monastery here in the 12th century; it was attached to the Cluniac order.

The church, which has a tall square tower to one side, forms an

enjoy an active break based on a wide range of sports e.g. tennis, golf, riding, trial motor bikes, sailing, windsurfing, swimming, angling in the R. Lignon, rambling, and cycling. In winter, there is cross-country skiing. The town hosts the International Cévenol College. It is traditionally a place of refuge and it won renown amont large numbers of refugees during the Second World War. The Chambon-sur-Lignon and Le Mazet-Saint-Voy areas remain staunchly Protestant.

Opposite : the village of Lavoûte-Chilhac.

Below : Château de Lavoûte-sur-Loire.

LE MONASTIER-SUR-GAZEILLE

This was the village chosen by Robert Louis Stevenson, the author of *Treasure Island*, as the starting point for his travels with a donkey through the Cévennes. The village is built around the ramparts of the oldest monastery in the Velay region (hence its name). The magnificent minster has mainly Romanesque architecture in the Burgundy style but with Gothic alterations. It contains a priceless 11th-century reliquary, the bust of St. Theofrede (or St. Chaffre). The museum has exceptionally extensive collections which are shown off to their best advantage; it is housed in the abbots' palace.

Nearby is the Récoumène Viaduct (260 ft.) which was used by those who enjoyed jumping from great heights attached to a long elastic rope.

*A bust of St. Theofred (or St. Chaffre)
in the abbey church in
Le Monastier-sur-Gazeille.*

Le-Puy-en-Velay, a wonderful setting.

LE PUY-EN-VELAY

This is a superb setting against a luxurious green backcloth of volcanic mountains in which water and fire have carved out natural beauty spots (Aiguilhe and Corneille Rocks, Mont Anis) and where Man has achieved the triumph of Beauty and Art.

The area was particularly suitable for prayer, fervent devotion and Christianity. With the departure of the Romans, churches were built here in the 4th century. The pilgrimage to Le Puy-Sainte-Marie continued to gain importance, reaching its height with the pilgrimage to pray to the famous Black Virgin during the Middle Ages.

The influence that spread through the Western Christian world was reinforced by the pilgrimages to Santiago de Compostela

The Italian Carnival in Le-Puy-en-Velay.

in Spain since Le Puy was one of the main gathering points in Europe (*Via Podiensis*). The first crusade preached by Pope Urban II in Clermont-Ferrand at the end of the 11th century had as its legate the Bishop of Le Puy, Adhemard de Monteil.

Popes, kings, and millions of pilgrims have come to pray in Notre-Dame Cathedral. Built in the Romanesque style with Arabic and Byzatine overtones brought from the East and the Spain of the Moors, half the building stands on rock; the other half stands on huge pillars built into the side of Mont Anis.

This remarkable piece of architecture is completed by polychrome cloisters (12th century), ornate capitals, a museum of religious art and the St. John Baptistery.

The upper town, with its narrow streets, flights of steps, coloured paving stones and houses (15th, 16th, 17th and 18th centuries) decorated with gables, turrets, mullioned windows, inner courtyards, and carved doors lies within an area of 35 hectares bordered by the old town walls. The entire area is covered by a protection order.

The Crozatier Museum, one of the most interesting museums outside Paris, stands within the Henri-Vinay Gardens. It houses fine collections of sculptures, paintings, and archaeology, as well as extensive collections relating to local history (lace, gold and silverware, archaeology etc.).

Proud of this prestigious history, Le-Puy-en-Velay has succeeded in developing into what is now a middle-sized but busy town (pop. 27,000) at the centre of a rural *département*. Its dynamic outlook is evident in its shops, crafts, services, cultural events and sports activities.

Numerous, and wide-ranging, events are scheduled throughout the year, the two main ones being the Italian-style carnival in March and the Bird-King Festival in mid-September which gives the town back the appearance and splendour of the Renaissance.

As a stopover or as a centre from which to tour a delightful region, Le-Puy-en-Velay is ideal for trips throughout Haute-Loire.

The town is also famous for its hand-made lace which has been made here for hundreds of years, using hand movements and techniques that have been preserved thanks to the setting up, in 1976, of a national lace workshop and academy which maintains the presence and the reality of this craft.

The "green lentils" produced in the 35 towns and villages in the vicinity of Le-Puy-en-Velay are a famous dish which even the greatest chefs have no hesitation in including in their recipes. And last but no least, the verbena liqueur known as "Verveine du Velay" has been famous since the 19th century.

The cloisters in Notre-Dame Cathedral in Le-Puy-en-Velay.

Le Mézenc, whose summit rises to 5,700 ft. In the distance are the Alps.

LES ESTABLES

A summer resort at an altitude of 4,374 ft. at the foot of Mont Mézenc (alt. 5,700 ft.), the highest peak in the *département*. A nordic region : cross-country skiing, downhill skiiing, rambling, and numerous sports activities e.g. parapente, mountain biking etc. Numerous varieties of mountain flowers. Superb panoramic view of the Alps.

MONTFAUCON-EN-VELAY

A popular tourist centre. Collection of 16th-century Flemish paintings in Notre-Dame church.

MONT-MOUCHET

Situated within the boundaries of Auvers, near Pinols. Once a centre for the Resistance Movement, HQ of Auvergne's FFI fighters. Museum.

MOUDEYRES

This village at the foot of Mont Mézenc still has a few traditional cottages, the most impressive being the Perrel Brothers' Farm (*Ferme des Frères Perrel*) which has become a listed traditional building. It is a museum of popular arts and traditions and bears witness to country life on the highland plateaus at the turn of the century.

Hot-air balloons above Polignac. The castle and its keep are clearly visible. In the distance is the Mézenc range.

The chapel of Sainte-Marie-des-Chazes between Prades and Saint-Julien-des-Chazes.

POLIGNAC

The incomparable view of Polignac remains in the memory of any visitor to Haute-Loire. The volcanic platform topped by a keep is 650 ft. in length and over 325 ft. wide. Set against the background of Mont Mézenc and the unique, Haute-Loire sky, it rises to 162 ft. above the village below. The castle, built on the site of a Temple of Apollo, is the home of the most illustrious family in the Velay region, the Polignacs, whose name has been closely linked to the history of Haute-Loire for one thousand years. The keep dates from the 15th century (with 19th-century restorations) and has a battlement walkway. The church in the centre of the village dates mainly from the Romanesque period. Nearby, in the hamlet of Bilhac, there is a wonderful crafts centre.

PEBRAC

A historic village known throughout the charming Desges Valley. One of the stops on the Poetry Festival Trail which, towards the end of the summer, brings to the attention of visitors the old abbey that is currently undergoing restoration.

PRADELLES

A strategic spot on the edges of the Velay, Vivarais, and Gévaudan regions, high above the Naussac Dam. The picturesque village was saved during the Wars of Religion by Jeanne la Verdette. It is a busy tourist centre, especially during the festival that is held every year at the end of July and that retells the eventful history of the region against the natural backcloth provided by the Renaissance houses in Pradelles.

PRADES

A popular tourist centre at the confluence of the rivers Seuge and Allier. Swimming and white water sports (raft, canoe, hydrospeed) at the foot of an area of columnar basalt. Nearby is the chapel of Notre-Dame d'Estours.

The ruins of the fortress stand high above the village of Chalençon.

RETOURNAC

Retournac in the Loire Valley is a busy town, the largest in the area, and it provides a wide range of leisure activities (swimming, tennis, canoeing, climbing, and camping on the river bank).

It is a good place from which to visit the surrounding area, in particular the ruins of the 11th-century feudal castle in Artias (3 miles).

SAINT-ANDRE-DE-CHALENCON

In Chalencon (1 mile from Saint-André) stand the ruins of the old fortress, high above the wild Ance Valley and the village. The ruins stand in a superb setting (10th-century tower, 12th-century Romanesque chapel) and the castle once belonged to the influential Chalencon family. The Devil's Bridge (*Pont du Diable*) is also worth a visit.

SAINT-ARCONS-D'ALLIER

A wonderful beauty spot between the Fioule and Allier Gorges. One of the high points on the Poetry Festival Trail. A superb example of village restoration carried out in a manner that respects the architectural heritage. Upmarket tourist accommodation is currently being prepared. The village includes a Tin Museum, the only one of its kind in France.

SAINT-FRONT

This mountain village (alt. 3,965 ft.) nestles round a magnificent little Romanesque church dominated by its gable-end belltower. The crater lake and the hamlet of Bigorre (cottages, unforgettable view of the blue horizons of Haute-Loire and, beyond, to the mountains of Auvergne) attract large numbers of visitors, as does the nordic area of Mont Mézenc.

The Tin Museum in Saint-Arcons-d'Allier.

SAINT-ILPIZE

The first, picturesque spot in the Upper Allier Tourist Route, after Vieille-Brioude. A superb beauty spot high above the river, linked to Villeneuve by a suspension bridge.

Castle ruins, Romanesque chapel.

SAINT-JULIEN-CHAPTEUIL

The birthplace of Louis Fargoule (1885-1973), better known under his pen-name, Jules Romains,who was born in the hamlet of La Chapuze. He was the author of such famous works as *Les Copains, Dr. Knock* and *Men of Good Will*. There is a Jules Romains Museum in a room in the Town Hall. Saint-Julien is a delightful beauty spot in the heart of the volcanic cone region. It is a busy town, popular with tourists, especially during the pageants held every year at the beginning of August. The event is a huge living fresco of local history.

The ruins of the castle in Saint-Ilpize.

SAINT-PAULIEN

A dynamic town, known to the Romans as *Ruessium*, the capital of the Vellavi tribe, built around the Auvergne-style Romanesque church (polychrome materials, apsidal chapels). Later alterations are obvious in the chapels and spire. Nearby, like a page from a fairy story, is Rochelambert Castle (15th and 16th centuries) which George Sand used as the setting for her novel, *Jean de la Roche*. It contains a wonderful collection of Romanesque statues of the Virgin Mary.

Château de la Rochelambert near Saint-Paulien.

SAINT-VIDAL

A picturesque town on the outskirts of Le-Puy-en-Velay, the setting every year, at the beginning of July, of a famous festival of music, drama and dance using the natural backcloth of the castle walls. The fortress is an exceptional 13th-16th century building with inner courtyard flanked by a gallery with ribbed vaulting, and a vast main hall with a stone doorway in the Italian Renaissance style.

SAINTE-SIGOLENE

This village has a population of 5,000 of which 1,700 are employed in the largest extruded polyethylene plant in France. The polyethylene is used for packaging. The traditional manufacturing industry, ribbon-making, has developed and now covers, in particular, the creation of scarves bearing the "Pierre Cardin" label.

The castle in Saint-Vidal.

SAUGUES

This is the main town in the Margeride area and it lies at the gateway to the Gévaudan. It is a

Saugues in the Margeride Region.

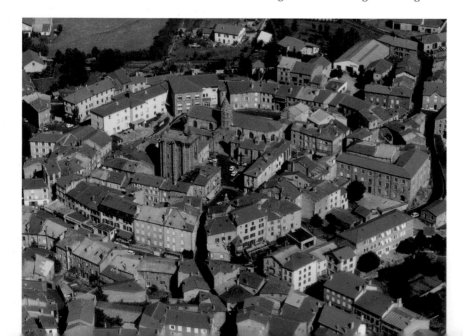

stopover for pilgrims travelling from Le-Puy-en-Velay to Santiago de Compostela (way-marked long-distance footpath GR 65). It is a delightful locality, made famous by Robert Sabatier in his book, *Les Noisettes Sauvages*, and, in the 18th century it became famous during the many hunts arranged to try and track down the Gévaudan Beast.

The Englishmen's Tower (*Tour des Anglais*) dates from the 12th century. The village of La Clauze has a strange 12th-century octagonal tower. The area shows the successful blend of water (rivers Seuge, Virlande, and Pontajou) and woodland (where mushrooms abound).

There is a project to set up the European Bison Park on the out-

Old Brioude.

skirts of Saugues on the edge of Haute-Loire, Cantal and Lozère.

TENCE

A popular tourist centre which attracts anglers because of the quality of the water in the R. Lignon (trout). The Place de Cha-tiague has a southern-French air about it and is backed by St. Martin's Church (Gothic chancel). This is the point of departure for numerous way-marked footpaths.

VALPRIVAS

This town, which lies on the borders of Loire and Haute-Loire, is now famous for its arts centre. For more than twenty years, the Valprivas Arts Centre Assocation has been working to restore the castle, much of which dates from the Renaissance, and to develop musical activities (concert programmes, music camps).

VIEILLE-BRIOUDE

It is at night that this spot at the confluence of the rivers Allier and Sénouire has to be seen for the first time. The particularly attractive floodlighting shows up the arch of the bridge, the church and the houses round about.

VOREY

A popular, small tourist centre at the confluence of the Arzon and Loire rivers, in the heart of the Emblavès region where the climate is particularly mild. Flume, swimming and fishing in the R. Loire. Nearby are the ruins of the 10th-century Roche-en-Régnier Fortress.

YSSINGEAUX

A sub-prefecture in the heart of the volcanic cone area and, since 1984, the seat of the National Pastrycooks' College (the only one in France). National and international training courses succeed one another in Montbarnier Castle, attracting numerous master pastrycooks to a town that was already famous for its buns. The town (pop. 7,000), which lies between the rivers Loire and Lignon, has a former Bishop's Palace that is now the Town Hall. It was built in the 15th century over a mediaeval fortress for Jean de Bourbon, Bishop of Le Puy, as a summer residence. For the past forty years, springtime has been celebrated in Yssingeaux by huge crowds who visit the town on carnaval day. There is a busy market on Thursdays.

Puy-de-Dôme

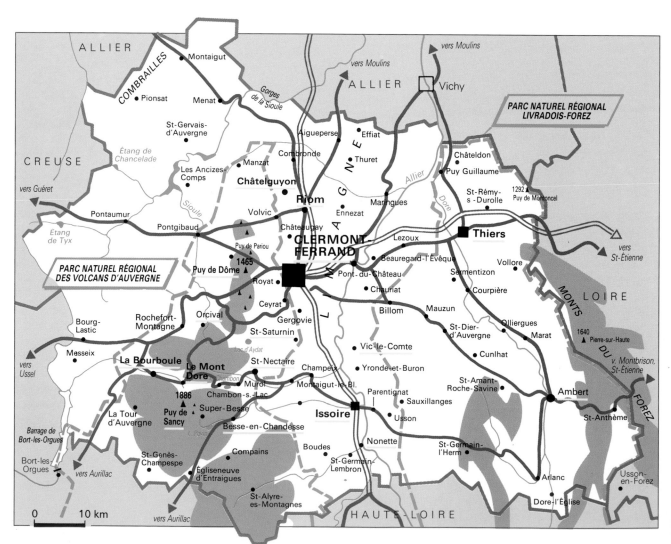

ALLIER

COMBRAILLES

Montaigut

vers Moulins

vers Moulins

ALLIER

Vichy

PARC NATUREL RÉGIONAL
LIVRADOIS-FOREZ

Pionsat

Menat

Gorges de la Sioule

Aigueperse

Effiat

Châteldon

CREUSE

St-Gervais-
d'Auvergne

Étang de
Chancelade

Combronde

Thuret

Puy Guillaume

Manzat

Allier

St-Rémy-
s-Durolle

1292 ▲
Puy de Montoncel

vers Guéret

Les Ancizes-
Comps

Châtelguyon

Sioule

Ennezat

Maringues

Dore

Pontaumur

Volvic

Riom

Pontgibaud

Châteaugay

Lezoux

Thiers

Étang
de Tyx

Puy de Pariou ▲

1465
Puy de Dôme ▲

CLERMONT-
FERRAND

Beauregard-l'Évêque

Vollore

vers
St-Étienne

PARC NATUREL RÉGIONAL
DES VOLCANS D'AUVERGNE

Royat

Ceyrat

Pont-du-Château

Chauriat

Sermentizon

Courpière

MONTS

LOIRE

Rochefort-
Montagne

Orcival

Gergovie

Billom

Mauzun

St-Dier-
d'Auvergne

Olliergues

Marat

DU

Bourg-
Lastic

St-Saturnin

1640
▲ Pierre-sur-Haute

Masseix

Lac d'Aydat

St-Nectaire

Vic-le-Comte

Yronde-et-Buron

Cunlhat

v. Montbrison,
St-Étienne

vers
Ussel

La Bourboule

Le Mont
Dore

Chambon

Murol

Champeix

Montaigut-le-Bl.

Parentignat

St-Amant-
Roche-Savine

Ambert

FOREZ

1886
Puy de
Sancy ▲

Chambon-s.-Lac

Super-Besse

Issoire

Sauxillanges

St-Anthème

La Tour
d'Auvergne

Besse-en-Chandesse

Usson

Barrage de
Bort-les-Orgues

L. Pavin

St-Genès-
Champespe

Compains

Boudes

Nonette

St-Germain-
l'Herm

Bort-les-
Orgues

Égliseneuve
d'Entraigues

St-Germain-
Lembron

Arlanc

Usson-
en-Forez

vers Aurillac

St-Alyre-
es-Montagnes

Dore-l'Église

0   10 km

vers Aurillac

HAUTE-LOIRE

AIGUEPERSE
(Grande Limagne)

The former capital of the Duchy of Montpensier has two unusual churches. The main one, the Collegiate Church of Notre-Dame, has a chancel with ambulatory and radiating chapels that is one of the earliest examples of Gothic architecture to be found in Auvergne. There are very fine frescoes dating from the late 13th and early 14th centuries (scenes from the Life of Christ, the martyrdom of St. Catherine) and two paintings of the Italian quattrocento period (Nativity scene). The former chapel of the Montpensier Palace, built in the Flamboyant Gothic style, contains statues of the Virgin Mary and St. Louis.

A few miles from Aigueperse is **Thuret**, which has a superb Romanesque church with three aisles. It is remarkable for its typanum depicting Christ in Majesty and its unusual carved capitals depicting, in particular, Adam and Eve.

In **Effiat**, there is a castle of majestic proportions that is typical of the architecture of the early 17th century. Its formal garden is still steeped in memories of Cinq-Mars, Marquis d'Effiat.

The Château de la Roche in **Chaptuzat** was the birthplace of Chancellor Michel de l'Hospital. Situated on a hill overlooking Aigueperse, the castle has an old Romanesque section combined with a main building that dates back to the Renaissance period.

AMBERT
(Livradois)

Ambert, which lies in a small clearing between the Forez Mountains and the Livradois area, is a small town which enjoyed a period of prosperity after the end

The Richard-de-Bas Mill Museum in Ambert.

of the Middle Ages thanks to its paper mills.

The Flamboyant Gothic cathedral is one of the few buildings of this type in the *département*. An inscription on the South Door serves as a reminder that Auvergne was the victim of earthquakes in the 15th century.

The Town Hall building was idealized by Jules Romains in his novel, *Les Copains*. It has an unusual shape, being round, because it was originally dsigned to be a grain store.

The Steam and Farm Machinery Museum (*AGRIVAP*) houses a collection of steam-powered traction engines and agricultural machinery.

A few minutes along the road is the very interesting Moulin-Richard-de-Bas Museum in which paper is still made using the techniques of days long gone.

Ambert's Puppet Festival is attracting increasingly large numbers of visitors to the town

every year at the beginning of August.

If you are in search of a general view of the region, try going up to the **Hautes Chaumes du Forez** from the Col des Supeyres or, better still, from the Pierre sur-Haute, the highest point. The remains of the old-style arable and pasture farming have left their marks on the landscape which includes a summer pasture hut and fields of heather on land reclaimed from the forest.

BEAUREGARD-L'EVEQUE
(Limagne)

For a long time, the town was the summer residence of the Bishops of Clermont. A few miles from the village, in Mirabeau, are the remains of the former Minim Convent, which was sold off as State property during the French Revolution and has since been used for farming.

Lake Pavin near Besse.

BESSE
(Monts Dore)

Situated in the heart of the Sancy uplands, Besse is, without doubt, the capital of the mountain region. It has retained several fine houses with stone-slabbed roofs, in particular "Queen Margot's House". It also has picturesque shop-lined streets dating from the 15th and 16th centuries (rue de la Boucherie).

The part-Romanesque church has several interesting capitals (e.g. the Evil Rich Man, and the Minotaur).

The town lies in the centre of the area which is entitled to name its cheese production "saint-nectaire". Every Monday, producers and manufacturers come together at the cheese market.

Super-Besse is one of the largest ski resorts in the Massif Central and has now been completed by Besse-Pavin where there is an internationally-famous nordic area.

The Water and Angling Centre enables tourists to see a trout hatchery and to find out about the natural environment through exhibitions and discovery trails.

One of the capitals in the church in Besse.

Not far from Besse is **Lake Pavin**, nestling in the heart of the most recent volcano in France. The lake has a mysterious atmosphere and its deep waters (more than 292 ft.) hide trout and chad.

The **Vassivière Chapel** not far from Besse is another place of pilgrimage.

BILLOM
(Bas Livradois)

A prestigious history linked to the university and, later, the college run by the Jesuit Order has left Billom an old urban district and the churches of St. Cerneuf and St. Loup.

The mediaeval district has not only the Rue des Boucheries and half-timbered houses; it also has a few interesting mansion houses such as the Dean of Guild's Mansion (*Maison de l'Echevin*), and the Deanery (*Maison du Doyen*) dating from the 15th and 16th centuries. The Deanery contains rich furnishings and numerous frescoes including the legend of St. Margaret (12th century) in the crypt, and the Coronation of the Virgin Mary and other scenes in the Rosary Chapel.

The surrounding countryside consists of gently rolling hills and gradually distinguishes itself from the Limagne. There are several churches that are worth a detour because they are examples of Early Romanesque architecture as it was understood in Auvergne e.g. Gaine-Montaigut, or Neuville.

Not far from Billom is **Montmorin Castle**, built in the latter years of the 12th century. Now carefully restored, it houses a collection of arms and armour, as well as other objects.

Top : Queen Margot's House in Besse.

Bottom : the old town in Billom.

Montmorin Castle near Billom.

CHAMALIERES

This town is well-known because it includes the Banque de France workshop and because a former President of the Republic (Valéry Giscard d'Estaing) was also its Mayor. Chamalières is the seat of Auvergne Regional Council. The church, once the Collegiate Church of Notre-Dame, dates from the 10th century and was altered in the 13th.

The modern art gallery managed by the painter, Slobo, organises remarkable exhibitions of paintings, tapestries and sculptures.

BOUDES
(Lembron Plain)

To the south of Issoire, the plain is a fertile agricultural area in which there is one high-quality vineyard, near **Boudes**. From the village, the road takes you to the Valley of Saints, so called because erosion has carved the clay and marl into human shapes and fairy chimneys.

High above the Lembron Plain is the Château de **Villeneuve-Lembron** which is especially interesting for its early 16th-century wall paintings illustrating the life of the then Lord of the Manor, Rigault d'Aureille. The frescoes dating from the second half of the 16th century illustrate the feats of the Montmorin family, through allegorical scenes (Perseus freeing Andromeda).

LA BOURBOULE
(Mont Dore)

This spa town lies on the banks of the Upper Dordogne and spe-

cialises in the treatment of respiratory disorders and skin allergies. It is much beloved of children who can take advantage of a magnificent play area in the Fenestre Park.

A cablecar leads up to the nearby Charlannes Plateau where there is a network of footpaths through the woodland.

Both spas offer visitors a wide range of coach tours leaving from the town.

CHAMBON-SUR-LAC
(Vallée Verte)

When the Tartaret Volcano closed off the end of the Couze Valley, it produced Lake Chambon which is now fully equiped to cater for tourists. In the village of Chambon, the graveyard has an unusual circular funeral chapel (12th century).

From the village of Chambon, the road leads to the **Chaudefour Valley**, a superb glacial valley

Chambon : Chaudefour Valley.

which is part of the Sancy uplands. It will probably be listed as a nature reserve over the coming months.

CHATELDON
(Bois Noirs)

The small town is worth a visit. It is a merchant town, which grew up around its castle, and it still has its beautiful half-timbered houses dating back to the 15th century in the Rue des Boucheries. The most outstanding are the "Sergeant's House" and the wine-producers' houses (18th century) in the Rue de l'Aire. A tiny tributary of the R. Allier, the Credogne, has gouged a picturesque valley out of the sides of the Dark Woods (*Bois Noirs*), forming a waterfall in the dip at Saillant.

CHATEL-GUYON
(Chaîne des Puys)

A few miles from Riom is the spa town of Châtel-Guyon, which is well-known for the treatment of liver complaints and intestinal disorders. In the immediate vicinity are the Prades Valley and the Sans-Souci Valley, both of which are pleasant places for a stroll. Among the most famous people to have been taken the waters in this town was Guy de Maupassant, who used it as the setting for his novel, *Mont Oriol*.

During the summer, the nearby Chazeron Castle stages musical evenings. It is a mediaeval building which underwent major alterations in the 17th century.

And last but not least, the area contains one of the most delightful crater lakes in Auvergne, the Gour de Tazenat, in Charbonnières-les-Vieilles.

St. Julian's Church in Chauriat.

CHAURIAT
(Limagne)

The Bishop of Clermot and the Count of Auvergne founded a priory here in the early years of the 11th century. St. Julian's Church has several interesting capitals (the Washing of the Disciples' Feet, the Multiplication of the Loaves), a Romanesque statue of the Virgin Mary in the chancel, and a transept built to the same layout as the largest churches in Auvergne.

Clermont-Ferrand : the cathedral and Place de la Victoire.

CLERMONT-FERRAND

The former capital of the Arverni tribe, now the regional capital of Auvergne and county town of the *département* of Puy-de-Dôme should not be seen as merely the centre of the tyre-making industry. Quite apart from the fact that the secondary sector has gradually shaken off the bounds of the single industry dominated by Michelin, and that the tertiary sector has become the main employer in the town, Cler-mont is also a tourist centre, offering visitors two towns of architectural interest viz. Clermont and Montferrand.

The town, which is black because of the colour of the Volvic stone used for its buildings, has gradually become more attractive thanks to the restoration of the old town which give visitors an opportunity to discover the delights and charms of Old Clermont. The Rue du Port, which was in fact the market, "*portus*", the Rue des Gras (i.e. the "*grad-ins* " or rows of seats) leading to the cathedral and the Rue des Chaussetiers all have a number of particularly interesting mansions. The Savaron Mansion in the Rue des Chaussetiers remains one of the most famous, with its elegant newel staircase leading up to three storeys of galleries and its carved tympanum over the front door.

The Cathedral, on the Place de la Victoire, was begun in 1248 and allies the Gothic style of Northern France to the use of Volvic stone. It replaced an older Romanesque cathedral dating from the 10th century of which only the crypt was retained. The building is remarkable for the quality of the stained glass in the chancel, the wonderful rose windows and the fenestration which let light into the transept.

Notre-Dame-du-Port, the most famous and arguably the finest example of Auvergnat Romanesque architcture, was built from the end of the 11th century onwards. It is built of arkose, a form of sandstone, and consists of three aisles, each with five spans, and four radiating chapels. The interior contains a veritable treasure trove e.g. an exceptional set of capitals carved by Maître Robertus including themes relating to the obedience of Mary and the disobedience of Eve.

Montferrand was finally annexed to Clermont in 1731. There are still numerous traces of the town that grew up thanks to the support of the Counts of Auvergne, in the face of opposition from the Bishop of Clermont. From the Place de la Rodade, there is a view of the Annunciation House (15th - 16th centuries), the Doyac Mansion, the Royal Bailiff's House, and the Court. The church of Notre-Dame-de-Prospérité (14th-15th centuries) is built in the Southern French Gothic style.

The town has a number of museums with interesting collections i.e. the Ranquet Museum in the Rue des Gras, the Bargoin Museum in the Rue Ballainvilliers, and the Lecoq Museum. The County Innovation Centre, the Conference Centre and the Arts Centre all house exhibitions or shows of many different kinds.

Finally, the short film festival, the "Sauve Qui Peut Le Court Métrage" has now become well-known through France.

Above : the Place de Jaude.

Below : Notre-Dame du Port, a masterpiece of Auvergnat Romanesque architecture.

COMPAINS
(Cézallier)

From **Brion**, there is a splendid panoramic view of the Cézallier area and the Mont Dore range. Yet as much as the scenery it is the cattle fairs that are held throughout the summer which are worth coming to see.

The "recent" volcanic activity has produced the Montcineyre Lake, at the foot of the volcano of the same name.

COURPIERE
(Dore Valley)

A few miles from Thiers, in the Dore Valley, lies Courpière. St. Martin's Priory Church is a Romanesque building and the village also has some wonderful half-timbered houses dating from the 15th century. The Order of the Knights of Malta set up a commandery in the hamlet of Courtesserre in the 15th century; all that remains today is the Gothic chapel.

On the lower slopes of the Forez is Vollore Castle, standing proudly above the Dore and Limagne Plains. It contains an interesting collection of memorabilia relating to General de Lafayette and also stages the Vollore concert season.

In **Aubusson-d'Auvergne**, the modest 15th-century church contains rich furnishings, in particular two polychrome wooden statues of the Virgin Mary dating from the Romanesque period. This area is currently being equiped for tourism and there is a lake in the Livradois-Forez Park.

La Godivelle Lake.

EGLISENEUVE d'ENTRAIGUES
(Monts Dore)

The village lies on the borders of the Cézallier and Artense areas. Every Wednesday, there is a major cheese market here. The Cheese Centre, housed in an old barn, shows visitors the techniques used to make saint-nectaire and some of the old tools once used. There is also a chance to taste the various cheeses made in Auvergne.

GERGOVIA

Although the name of the battle during which the Chief of the

Montcineyre Lake near Compains.

Arverni, Vercingetorix, defeated Julius Caesar in 52 B.C. has remained famous, the exact site of the battle is open to controversy. Gergovia, which was recognised by Napoleon III, vies with the hillfort on the hills of Clermont for this honour. Each side, of course, has its supporters. The parish of La Roche-Blanche which includes most of the Gergovia Plateau intends to set up a Gergo-

rance, Issoire has based its expansion on easy links between plain and mountain. The Sainte-Paule Fair still attracts large numbers of farmers. The town's present expansion is based on the aluminium industry, with the PUK Group which works in the aeronautics sector (Concorde, Airbus).

Despite an eventful past, especially during the Wars of Religion when the town was a Protestant

five radiating chapels and, above all, the carved capitals, the most famous of which illustrates the Last Supper.

A few miles away, in **Parentignat**, visitors can see the "Little Versailles of Auvergne", laid out in the 18th century by the Lastic family, to whom it still belongs. The house has a large quantity of period furniture (tapestries, paintings).

Château de Ravel near Lezoux.

via Centre specialising in history, archaeology and the battle field, and including discovery trails.

ISSOIRE
(Southern Limagne)

Situated in the heart of the Southern Limagne, in an open landscape with a Southern-French appea-

stronghold, it has retained the largest of the main churches in the Limagne region. The Church of St. Austremoine, named after the first Bishop of Auvergne, is as remarkable for its magnificent apse decorated with coloured-stone mosaics that include the signs of the zodiac on the radiating chapels, as it is for the long seven-spanned nave, the chancel and its

LEZOUX
(Varennes Region)

On the edge of the Limagne area is the Varennes Region, an area of infertile clay and sand. **Lezoux** enjoyed a period of prestige during the days of the Roman Conquest. In the 1st and 2nd centuries A.D. it was the largest centre of production of sigillated pottery.

The archaeology museum, indeed, contains the Gallic and Gallo-Roman pottery discovered during successive digs. Not far from Lezoux is **Ravel** which has two buildings of interest i.e. its 13th-century Gothic church and, more importantly, the chateau from which there is a superb panoramic view of the Limagne region and the Puy range.

This area of poor soil is particularly suitable for forestation. The Randan Forest on the edge of the Bourbonnais area is a fine example, with its 2,000 hectares of deciduous trees and conifers.

MANGLIEU

The monastery founded in the 7th century by St. Genès, Bishop of Clermont is well worth taking time to visit. At the entrance, beneath the triumphal arch, are Roman columns which have been re-used and topped by Merovingian capitals. The 12th-century Galilee porch should have marked the start of the rebuilding of the church but only the nave was rebuilt, in the 16th century.

MARINGUES
(Varennes Region)

This small town has kept alive memories of its erstwhile tanning industry with the restoration of the Grande Tannerie and the Tannerie Grandval. The Grande Tannerie is a 17th and 18th-century building with four storeys used for the treatment and drying of hides.

Maringues is a busy little town with a regular influx of people on Mondays, when the poultry market is held.

Not far away is Montgaçon, a feudal motte rising high above the Limagne Plain.

MAUZUN
(Lower Livradois)

The superb Mauzun Castle dates from the 12th century, although the site had been fortified since the days of Antiquity, in particular to afford protection for the Roman road that ran through Billom, Neuville and Sermentizon. In the 13th century, the castle became the property of the Bishops of Clermont who used it first as their residence and later as an ecclesiastical prison. An association is now trying to raise the castle from its ruins.

MENAT
(Lower Combraille)

Menat, on the edge of the Sioule Valley in Lower Combraille, has a very interesting geographical situation in a dip that has been filled with fossilised flora and fauna for thousands of years.

Nowadays, a Paleontology Museum called the Gîte à Fossiles gives visitors an opportunity to admire some remarkable collections of fossils preserved in schist.

The church replaced a very old Benedictine monastery which was founded in the 6th century.

Above : Mauzun Castle.

Opposite : Château-Rocher in Menat.

Menat Bridge is said to be very old. High above it are the impressive ruins of Rocher Castle, which is currently being restored by a youth heritage project.

The Bois des Brosses menhir is a noteworthy standing stone weighing approximately 8 tonnes for a length of over 14 ft.

111

LE MONT-DORE
(Monts Dore)

The spa town of Mont-Dore at the foot of the Sancy Uplands makes use of water whose properties were already known in Roman times. This was also one of the earliest French ski resorts; with Chamonix.

The **Puy de Sancy** (alt. 6,129 ft.) is the highest peak in the Massif Central and is one of the stratovolcanoes in the Monts Dore. There is a cablecar to the summit.

Nearby, there are a number of beauty spots that are worth a visit, in particular the Grande Cascade or other, smaller waterfalls at Le Queureuille and Le Saut du Loup.

MUROL
(Vallée Verte)

Murol, standing on its spur of basalt, is no longer the warring fortress of Guillaume de Murol. However, the castle has been brought back to life through the remarkable show staged by a troup of actor-stuntmen called "Les Compagnons de Gabriel" who welcome the public in a truly mediaeval atmosphere.

NONETTE
(Lembron Plain)

The river that drains the Lembron Plain, the Couze d'Ardes, flows into the Allier at Le Breuil-sur-Couze at the foot of **Nonette Hill.** The rise consists of a volcanic dyke from which there is a magnificent panoramic view of the entire area. Little is left of the castle built for Jean de Berry in the 14th century. The church is interesting for its decorative features and its West Door, its capitals and a bust of Christ.

Mont-Dore.

The Tuilière and Sanadoire Rocks in Orcival.

ORCIVAL
(Monts Dore)

Orcival, on the edge of the Monts Dore uplands, has **one of the finest churches in the region**. Built in the 12th century on the site of an older sanctuary, it is famous for the pilgrimage that still arouses the same deep fervour today. The church was built on a reverse gradient, facing the mountain. Even though the apse is plain and austere, it is still attractive for its layout. Because of the setting, the nave is smaller and encloses the narthex. The chevet has an ambulatory and four radiating chapels. A 12th-century statue of the Virgin Mary in Majesty, covered with gold, escaped damage during the French Revolution.

Not far away is the **Château de Cordès**, dating partly from the 15th century. The arbours in its park were designed by Le Nôtre.

The road to the Col de Guéry passes through some of the most beautiful scenery in Auvergne, containing the **Tuilière and Sanadoire Rocks**. Two volcanic rocks flank a bowl-shaped valley which has been partially cleared by glacial erosion. The Roche-Tuilière, known as a phonolith, can be cut into slabs and has provided roofing material for houses in the neighbourhood. As to the Roche-Sanadoire, it was used as a

The 12th-century statue of the Virgin Mary in Majesty in Orcival church.

During the summer, the castle is used for a music festival; throughout the year it houses exhibitions.

The tiny church nearby, in **Vergheas** (12th century) contains a copy of a 13th-century statue of the Virgin Mary (the original was stolen).

This is also an area of lakes of all sizes, including Tyx (67 hectares) and Chancelade.

The expansion of the tourist industry in Les Combrailles is partly due to the facilities provided in the Fades-Besserve Reservoir. There is also a view of the Fades Viaduct, the highest railway viaduct in Europe, standing 432 ft. above the R. Sioule.

PONTGIBAUD
(Chaîne des Puys)

Pontgibaud lies at the western end of the Puys Range. St. Benedict's Church (*église Saint-Benoît*) has interesting furniture which was brought here from the Carthusian monastery in Port-Sainte-Marie on the banks of the Sioule. The monastery was sold off and demolished after the French Revolution. Château-Dauphin was built in the 12th century but has undergone major alterations since that time.

Silver lead mines were worked here until the 19th century. Tradition has it that specks of gold dust could even be seen in the R. Sioule.

Puy de Dôme : the head office of the Volcano Park.

refuge by brigands and English mercenaries during the One Hundred Years' War.

Two lakes produced by volcanic activity are now very popular with tourists. **Servières Lake**, an explosive throat with an area of some 16 hectares, lies in the midst of pine forests and pasture.

The 25-hectare **Guéry Lake** is a dam which lies in scenery dominated by the Sancy range. Landscape and Botany Trails have been set up by the Parc des Volcans to enable visitors to discover the rich diversity of this spot.

PIONSAT
(Les Combrailles)

Pionsat, in the heart of the pastures and hedgerows of the Combrailles area, has a castle with one old wing dating partly from the 14th century and main apartments dating from the 16th.

114

Hang-gliders above the Puy de Dôme.

Near Pontgibaud, in Montfermy, the tiny Romanesque church contains an outstanding set of murals.

PONT-DU-CHATEAU
(Limagne)

Not far from Clermont-Ferrand on the RN 89 road lies Pont-du-Château, for many years the only permanent crossing point on the R. Allier. The local noblemen, in particular the Montboissier Beaufort Canillac family, drew much of their income from this situation.

River traffic was known to have existed very early in the history of Pont-du-Château. It enjoyed major expansion after the Briare Canal came into service in 1664, when the produce of Auvergne could be taken by boat to the markets of Paris.

The Riverboat Museum below the castle, on the Place de l'Aire, explains the ins-and-outs of this trade.

The castle that once belonged to the Canillac-Montboissiers is now used as the town hall. It still has its fine frontage with a main staircase, and two wonderful French-style ceilings.

St. Martine's Church is high above the R. Allier and the Marine District. It has a delightful narthex built in the Romanesque style.

LE PUY DE DOME

Honour where honour's due. The highest volcano (alt. 4,761 ft.) in the Puys Range has become the symbol of both the *département* with the same name and Auvergne as a whole. It is also a highly-prized site and there are numerous projects centring on this prestigious location. It is now one of the most popular places in France, as a result of the lively overnight stops on the Tour de France cycle race and the experiments carried out here by Pascal.

In the past, this was a sacred place. A Temple of Mars was built here in the 1st century B.C. and it also had a huge bronze sta-

115

tue cast by a Greek sculptor name Zenodore. Nowadays, only the foundations of the temple are left.

RIOM
(Grande-Limagne)

The old judicial town fully merits its nickname, "Riom the Beautiful". Its prestigious history has left it with remarkable urban architecture.

St. Amable's Church, whose relics are still the object of an annual procession, contains a fine collection of liturgical ornaments

The Sainte-Chapelle in Riom.

dating from before the French Revolution. The Collegiate Church of Le Marthuret (14th century) houses the famous statue of the **Virgin Mary with the Bird**.

The Sainte-Chapelle, which was commissioned in the second half of the 14th century by Jean de Berry, is remarkable for its Flamboyant Gothic architecture. Although the stained glass windows have been damaged and remounted in a rather unusual manner, they still constitute an exceptional collection.

The **Mandet Museum** recently acquired the Richard Donation. Set

out in two private mansions, it contains paintings from the Flemish, Dutch and French schools of the 17th, 18th and 19th centuries.

The **Auvergne Regional Museum** has traditional costumes and tools from Upper and Lower Auvergne.

A stroll through the town reveals numerous houses dating from the period between the 16th and 19th centuries e.g. the Soubrany Residence, the Consuls' Residence, the Guymoneau Mansion and the Chabre Residence.

In the immediate vicinity of Riom is **Mozac** which, until the earthquake of the late 15th century, had one of the finest Romanesque churches in Auvergne. Now it has a fine set of capitals carved with illustrations of various scenes from the fantasy-filled bestiary, and an enamelled reliquary of St. Calmin (12th century).

In summer, Riom stages an excellent piano festival. The Agency of the Traditional Music of Auvergne has set up its head office in the town.

ROYAT

Royat is a spa town that has had a high reputation since the Middle Ages for the treatment of heart disease, arterial disorders and arthritis. The old town contains a beautiful fortified Romanesque church standing on a lava flow. A semi-precious stonecutters' workshop (amethysts, agathas) is open to the public.

SAINT-AMANT-ROCHE-SAVINE
(Upper Livradois)

Saint-Amant-Roche-Savine lies in the heart of the highlands of the Livradois, in the land where Gaspard of the Mountains was said to have lived. It has a 15th-century Gothic church containing interesting furnishings, some of which are listed items in their own right (e.g. statue of the Virgin Mary), and there are several particularly attractive houses. The village now organises an unusual festival, inviting a number of rock bands to attend the "Saint-Amant-Rocke-ça-vibre" Festival at the beginning of August.

To the north of Saint-Amant is the "Toutée Observation Platform" from which there is a superb panoramic view of an area of forest that used to be the home of pit-sawyers.

SAINT-ALYRE-ESMONTAGNES
(Cézallier)

This is the home of the peat bog centre called **Rossolis**, which was set up with the backing of the Volcano Park. Visitors can walk across the peat bog in the Jacquot Plain on a pontoon and discover more about the ecology of the area in the information centre.

A peat bog in **La Godivelle** has been turned into a natural conservancy area.

SAINT-DIER-D'AUVERGNE
(Lower Livradois)

Saint-Dier-d'Auvergne, in the heart of a small basin, has an interesting fortified church built of sandstone (or arkosic sandstone, to be more precise) whose West Front is particularly well-finished. The interior is outstanding for its triple-spanned nave and semi-circular chevet opening directly onto three radiating chapels.

The nearby Château des Martinaches was built early in the 16th century on the remains of an old fortress. It has an attractive formal garden.

The village of Saint-Floret.

SAINT-FLORET
(La Couze Pavin Valley)

This delightful little village in the narrow Couze Pavin Valley has a castle containing some 14th-century remarkable frescoes telling the tale of Tristan and Yseult. Le Chastel Church on a promontory high above the village has a 15th-century mural and a mediaeval graveyard with an ossuary. There are also numerous coffins carved directly into the rock.

The church in Saint-Nectaire.

SAINT-GENES-CHAMPESPE
(Artense)

In the very centre of the Artense area is a magnificent observation platform providing a circular panoramic view; it is the mound on which the church is built. The countryside has a wild appearance marked by glacial erosion. Numerous lakes and ponds are dotted throughout this area, e.g. in La Crégut or Laspialade.

SAINT-GERMAIN-L'HERM
(Upper Livradois)

In Saint-Germain-L'Herm (alt. 3,412 ft.), in the midst of the pine trees, monks from La Chaise-Dieu founded a priory in the 11th century. The priory church has undergone several alterations but still has a few Romanesque features including the archaic style capitals in the transept. The town has also laid great store on entertainments by developing an arts and cultural festival in mid-August.

Not far away, in Saint-Bonnet-le-Bourg, there is a Craft Centre which exhibits and sells items made during the low season.

SAINT-NECTAIRE
(Vallée Verte)

Saint-Nectaire is an attractive, well-equiped tourist centre. Lying in the Upper Couze Chambon Valley, Saint-Nectaire has one of the five most beautiful Romanesque churches in Auvergne. Built in the 12th century, it has the same layout as the other major churches in the region, with a narthex preceding the three aisles, a projecting transept, a chevet with ambulatory and, from the outside, a chevet of uniform design. The chancel and nave are decorated with numerous carved, painted capitals retelling stories, some of which were carved in Notre-Dame-du-Port in Clermont-Ferrand. The church treasure has a bust-reliquary of St. Baudime made of wood and covered with gilded copper (12th century).

Saint-Nectaire-le-Bas is a small spa town specialising in liver complaints and metabolism disorders.

118

SAINT-REMY-SUR-DUROLLE
(Bois Noirs)

Saint-Rémy-sur-Durolle, a few miles from Thiers on the upland plateaus of Bois Noirs, has developed a cutlery industry specialising in the manufacture of penknives.

A small lake is suitable for a variety of water sports.

From the nearby Puy de Montoncel, there is an all-round panoramic view of the neighbouring mountain ranges. In this area, known as the Dark Woods (*Bois Noirs*), peat bogs have developed in basins caused by glacial overdeepening.

SAINT-SATURNIN
(Veyre Valley)

Situated on the edges of lava flows from the Puy Range and on the borders of the Veyre and Monne Valleys, the villages in this area are all worth a visit.

Clinging onto the edge of a basalt ridge, **Saint-Saturnin** still has a mediaeval appearance with its old houses in the Rue des Nobles or the Rue des Boucheries. The castle, once the residence of the Barons de la Tour d'Auvergne, has a 13th-century central section with later alterations. The facade dates from the Renaissance period, as does the fountain nearby.

The church, although the smallest of the major churches in the Limagne area, is remarkable. Built in the 12th century, its walls are made of the local blonde arkosic sandstone. The two-storey belltower has survived the storms of successive revolutions. A crypt has been laid out beneath the church and contains a fine 15th-century Pietà made of painted limestone.

The neighbouring village of **Saint-Amant-Tallende**, a former Stone Age graveyard, has a few interesting traces of its past, in particular a delightful bridge over the R. Monne. This commercial town began to develop its fairs and markets in the 19th century.

Not far away, nature lovers can enjoy the footpaths that lead into the **Monne Gorge** where the landscape is wild and rugged. High above them, they will see the recently-built Randol Abbey.

In **Olloix**, once the seat of a Commandery of the monk-soldiers of the Order of the Knights Templar, the church contains a recumbent statue of Odon of Montaigu, Prior of the Knights Hospitallers of Auvergne.

Overleaf : the Salt Spring Valley near La Tour-d'Auvergne.

Below : the church and fountain in Saint-Saturnin.

LA TOUR D'AUVERGNE
(Monts Dore)

In La Tour-d'Auvergne on the south-western slopes of the Monts Dore range, little remains of the formidable fortress that once belonged to the family of the same name. Only the church square is worthy of interest. The statue of the Virgin Mary in the church of Notre-Dame-de-Natzy is the destination of a major pilgrimage at the beginning of August. St. Pardoux' Church is the setting for high-quality Musical Days every summer.

In Picherande, a few miles away, the village of La Morangie stands at the entrance to the superb glacial **Salt Spring Valley** (*Vallée de la Fontaine Salée*) which to date has escaped several major development projects.

SERMENTIZON

Aulteribe Castle stands above a narrow ravine. Built in the 15th century and, later subjected to numerous alterations, it is particularly interesting for its rich furnishings and its gallery of paintings in which every period is represented. In Sermentizon itself, the bell-tower and entrance to the graveyard were rebuilt in the 19th century in the Florentine style.

THIERS
(Thiers Region)

Because of its wonderful location close to the western slopes of the Bois Noirs and adjacent to the Limagne area, the town of Thiers stands on a scarp slope along the fault line. Originally built in the lower district around Le Moutier, it developed around St. Genès' Church and the castle of the Lords of Thiers. Nowadays, the town is undergoing reverse expansion, with a tendency to displace its centre of gravity downwards towards the plain.

Thiers owes its prosperity to cutlery, and has done so since the end of the Middle Ages, in a region which has, for many years, been the focal point of local industry.

The castle in Yronde-et-Buron.

The Man of the Woods House in Thiers.

The present-day **Cutlery Centre** illustrates the richness of this industrial heritage and continues to produce upmarket cutlery in front of visitors.

The Symposium of monumental metal sculpture has perpetuated this tradition of metal-working through the artists who have

set up their works in the town. The "Creux de l'Enfer" (literally "Hell-hole") has been turned into a Modern Art Gallery.

Beyond the "World's End" (*Bout du Monde*) in the Durolle Valley, the remains of "**wheels**" can still be seen in each village, where they were installed for the knife-grinders and polishers. The "Thiers Region" organises tours of this valley of grinding wheels.

The old town is full of interest for sightseers, with its winding streets and half-timbered houses. The Rue de la Coutellerie has a large number of typical old houses, in particular the Man of the Woods' House (15th century), the famous Le Pirou Residence, home of the town's governors, and the House of the Seven Deadly Sins whose beams are carved with allegorical figures.

St. Genès' Church is a former collegiate church dating from the 11th century and has undergone alteration on many occasions since then. The Auvergne-style external decoration is interesting, with its billet-moulding and mosaics of polychrome stonework.

USSON
(Limagne)

In **Usson**, which is filled with memories of Queen Margot who spent more than twenty years here, there is no longer any trace of the mighty fortress described by Guillaume de Revel in his armorial. The part-Romanesque church, however, contains two outstanding works of art, one of them by the Flemish school (late 15th century) and the other by a Swiss painter named Deutsch (early 16th century). The Pic d'Usson, with its columnar basalt, provides a superb view of the region as a whole.

VIC-LE-COMTE
(Comté)

The Comté region, lying between the Allier Valley and the mountains in Livradois, is a delightful area with rugged landscapes caused by volcanic activity in the Tertiary Era that gave rise to a wide variety of scenery. Vic-le-Comte was, for many years, the capital of the small County of Auvergne. From this period, it has retained the Sainte-Chapelle built by John Stuart in the early 16th century (the chancel and chevet in the church as it is today) and St. John's Church which contains 14th-century frescoes.

The region is full of castles, all of them on scarp slopes. Bosséol Castle stands proudly on an outcrop of basalt. It has a Romanesque fireplace with a circular mantle and a small hanging garden on a terrace.

VOLVIC
(Chaîne des Puys)

Volvic has become the "Town of Stone and Water". Now famous for the mineral water of the same name, whose springs are open to the public, Volvic owed its prosperity from the Middle Ages onwards to the quarrying of stone. Numerous buildings, including the cathedral in Clermont or town houses in Riom, show the successful use of this building material.

The **Stone Centre** was set up by the Volcano Park in an old underground quarry within the lava flow from the Puy de la Nugère.

In addition to St. Priest's Church (12th century) which has a fine chevet with ambulatory and radiating chapels, and the Sahut Museum of Art, the most popular location with tourists is **Tournoël Castle**. This impressive fortress stands proudly on a promontory. It has two sets of fortifications, one dating from the 12th century, the other from the 14th and 15th centuries. The castle was damaged during the Wars of Religion and is now being restored by the family of the famous film-director, Chabrol.

YRONDE-ET-BURON

Buron Castle in Yronde-et-Buron lies in ruins. The local noblemen had a terrible reputation for being brigands. One of them gave rise to the legend of Garou, which is illustrated on the vaulted roof in the village chapel. Further downhill towards the R. Allier, there are the ruins of the old Le Bouschet Abbey, which was destroyed during the French Revolution.

The village of **Montpeyroux** stands opposite Yronde-et-Buron,

on a mound overlooking the confluence of the Allier and the Couze Chambon. This fortified village, with its 13th-century keep, has been very well-preserved. It has houses built of arkosic sandstone.

Auvergne is ideal for winter sports.
Our photo shows a group of skiers on the Mont Dore.

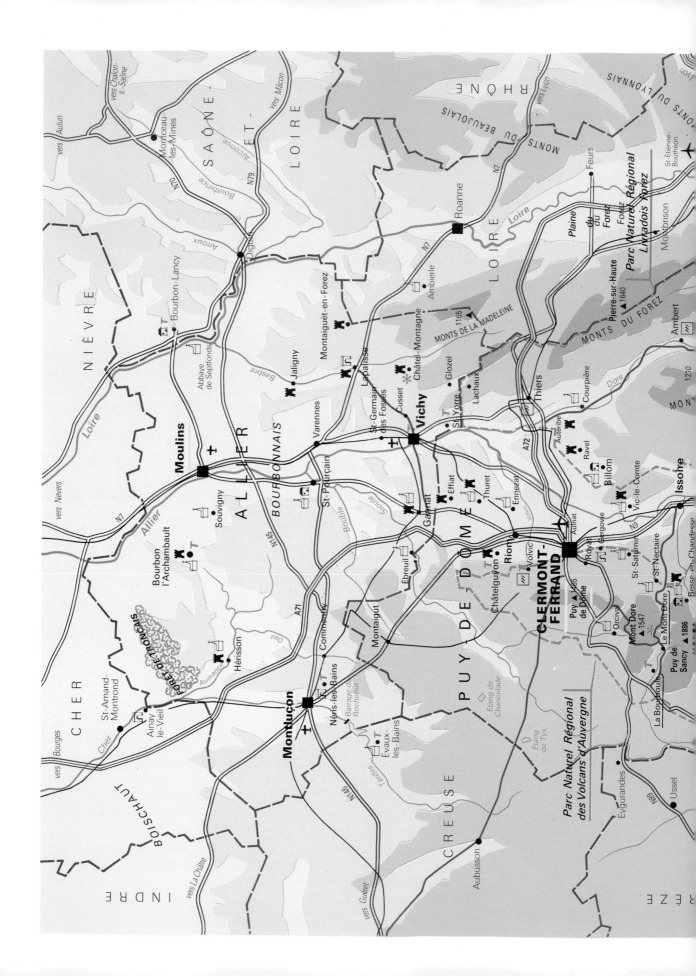